Access to History:
General Editor: Robert Pearce

Fascism and Nazism

Robert Pearce

Hodder & Stoughton
A MEMBER OF THE HODDER HEADLINE GROUP

The cover illustration is a photograph of Hitler and Mussolini (reproduced courtesy of Popperfoto)

British Library Cataloguing in Publication Data

A catalogue for this book is available in the British Library

ISBN 0-340-67964-6

First published 1997

Impression number	10	9	8	7	6	5	4	3	2	1
Year	2002		2001		2000		1998		1997	

Typeset by Sempringham publishing services, Bedford
Printed in Great Britain for Hodder & Stoughton Educational,
a division of Hodder Headline Plc, 338 Euston Road, London NW1 3BH
by Redwood Books, Trowbridge, Wiltshire

Contents

Acknowledgements

The publishers would like to thank the following for permission to reproduce the following copyright illustrations:

Cover - a photograph of Hitler and Mussolini (courtesy of Popperfoto). Weidenfeld and Nicolson Archive, p. 45; The Wiener Library, London, p. 79; David King Collection p. 102; David Low in the Evening Standard 28 August 1937, p. 87; David Low in the *Evening Standard* 5 February 1938, p. 115; David Low in the *Evening Standard* 27 June 1933, p. 116 (top); David Low in the *Evening Standard* 3 August 1934, p. 116 (bottom): Low cartoons supplied by Centre for the Study of Cartoons and Caricature, University of Kent at Canterbury.

The publishers would like to thank the following for permission to reproduce material in this volume:

Addison Wesley Longman for an extract from *Left and Right in Twentieth-Century Europe* by D. Smith (1970); Batsford for extracts from *The Rise of Fascism* by F.L. Carsten (1967); Cambridge University Press for an extract from *Fascist Italy and Nazi Germany* Richard Bessel (ed) and *The Racial State: Germany 1933-1945* by M. Burleigh and W. Wipperman; Bantam Press, a division of Transworld Publishers for an extract from *Millennium* by Felipe Fernández-Armesto © Felipe Fernández-Armesto. Cape for an extract from *Hitler and I* (1940) by O. Strasser; Chatto & Windus for an extract from *Fascism: A History* by R. Eatwell (1995); Coronet for an extract from *Hitler* by N. Stone (1982); Flamingo for an extract from *Hitler: The Führer and the People* by J.P. Stern (1984); Fontana for an extract from *The Rome-Berlin Axis* by E. Wiskemann (1966); Grafton Books for an extract from *By-line: Selected Articles and Dispatches of Four Decades* by E. Hemingway (1968); Hamish Hamilton for an extract from *Looking for Trouble* by V. Cowles (1941); Heinemann for an extract from *Modern European History, 1871-1975: A Documentary Reader* by D. Welch (1994) and *Ciano's Diary* by M. Muggeridge (ed.); Macmillan for an extract from *Fascism* by M. Kitchen (1976), *Italian Fascism 1919-1945* by P. Morgan (1995), *National Socialism in Germany* by N. Rothnie (1987), *A History of the Jews in the English-Speaking World: Great Britain* by W. Rubenstein (1995) and *The Nazi Economic Recovery, 1932-38* by R.J. Overy, *Twenty Years' Crisis* by E.H. Carr (1946); Nelson for an extract from *My Life* by Sir Oswald Mosley (1968); Oxford University Press for an extract from *Hitler's Table-Talk* by H. Trevor-Roper (ed) (1988) and *Fascism* by R. Griffin (1995); Penguin Books Ltd for extracts from *Essays, Journalism and Letters* of George Orwell, Vol. 3, (1970), *Thus Spake Zarathustra* by F. Nietzsche (Penguin edition, 1961), *The English Ideology* by G. Watson (1973), *Nineteen Eighty-Four* by G. Orwell (1954) and *Hitler: A Study in Tyranny* by A. Bullock (1962); Routledge for an extract from *The Nature of Fascism* by R. Griffin (1991); the Historical Association for extracts from *Fascism in Europe, 1919-1945* by R.A.H. Robinson; UCL Press for an extract from *A History of Fascism 1914-45* by S.G. Payne (1995); Van Nostrand for extracts from *Varieties of Fascism* by E. Weber (1964); Weidenfeld and Nicolson for extracts from *European Fascism* S.J. Woolf (ed) (1968) and *Three faces of Facsisim* by E. Nolte (1966).

Every effort has been made to trace and acknowledge ownership of copyright. The publishers will be glad to make suitable arrangements with any copyright holders whom it has not been possible to contact.

Preface

The original *Access to History* series was conceived as a collection of sets of books covering popular chronological periods in British history, such as 'The Tudors' and 'the nineteenth century', together with the histories of other countries, such as France, Germany, Russia and the USA. This arrangement complemented the way in which early-modern and modern history has traditionally been taught in sixth forms, colleges and universities. In recent years, however, other ways of dividing up the past have become increasingly popular. In particular, there has been a greater emphasis on studying relatively brief periods in considerable detail and on comparing similar historical phenomena in different countries. These developments have generated a demand for appropriate learning materials, and, in response, two new 'strands' are being added to the main series - *In Depth* and *Themes*. The new volumes build directly on the features that have made *Access to History* so popular.

To the general reader

Although *Access* books have been specifically designed to meet the needs of examination students, these volumes also have much to offer the general reader. *Access* authors are committed to the belief that good history must not only be accurate, up-to-date and scholarly, but also clearly and attractively written. The main body of the text (excluding the Study Guides) should, therefore, form a readable and engaging survey of a topic. Moreover, each author has aimed not merely to provide as clear an explanation as possible of what happened in the past but also to stimulate readers and to challenge them into thinking for themselves about the past and its significance. Thus, although no prior knowledge is expected from the reader, he or she is treated as an intelligent and thinking person throughout. The author tends to share ideas and explore possibilities, instead of delivering so-called 'historical truths' from on high.

To the student reader

It is intended that *Access* books should be used by students studying History at a higher level. Its volumes are all designed to be working texts, which should be reasonably clear on a first reading but which will benefit from re-reading and close study.

To be an effective and successful student, you need to budget your time wisely. Hence you should think carefully about how important the material in a particular book is for you. If you simply need to acquire a general grasp of a topic, the following approach will probably be effective:

1 Read Chapter 1, which should give you an overview of the whole book, and think about its contents.
2 Skim through Chapter 2, paying particular attention to the opening section and to the headings and sub-headings. Decide if you need to read the whole chapter.
3 If you do, read the chapter, stopping at the end of every sub-division of the text to make notes.
4 Repeat stage 2 (and stage 3 where appropriate) for the other chapters.

If, however, your course - and your particular approach to it - demands a detailed knowledge of the contents of the book, you will need to be correspondingly more thorough. There is no perfect way of studying, and it is particularly worthwhile experimenting with different styles of note-making to find the one that best suits you. Nevertheless, the following plan of action is worth trying:

1 Read a whole chapter quickly, preferably at one sitting. Avoid the temptation - which may be very great - to make notes at this stage.
2 Study the flow diagram at the end of the chapter, ensuring that you understand the general 'shape' of what you have read.
3 Re-read the chapter more slowly, this time taking notes. You may well be amazed at how much more intelligible and straightforward the material seems on a second reading - and your notes will be correspondingly more useful to you when you have to write an essay or revise for an exam. In the long run, reading a chapter twice can, in fact, often save time. Be sure to make your notes in a clear, orderly fashion, and spread them out so that, if necessary, you can later add extra information.
4 Read the advice on essay questions, and do tackle the specimen titles. (Remember that if learning is to be effective, it must be active. No one - alas - has yet devised any substitute for real effort. It is up to you to make up your own mind on the key issues in any topic.)
5 Attempt the source-based questions. The guidance on tackling these exercises, which is generally given at least once in a book, is well worth reading and thinking about.

When you have finished the main chapters, go through the 'Further Reading' section. Remember that no single book can ever do more than introduce a topic, and it is to be hoped that - time permitting - you will want to read more widely. If *Access* books help you to discover just how diverse and fascinating the human past can be, the series will have succeeded in its aim - and you will experience that enthusiasm for the subject which, along with efficient learning, is the hallmark of all the best students.

Robert Pearce

CHAPTER 1

Introduction: The Problem of Fascism

In 1918, at the end of a brutal and exhausting war, many Europeans were determined that another such conflict should never occur again. The Great War must be 'the war to end war'. Militarism was to be outlawed, state boundaries were to be redrawn to take account of national identity, and the world was to be made safe for democracy. Optimists believed that Europe was about to enter an era of peace, prosperity and respect for human rights. The future would surely be the best of times. Yet 20 years later such hopes seemed childishly naive. By then, one state after another had given way to authoritarian rule and a second world war was about to be unleashed. For many, it was the worst of times - and the chief culprit was fascism. (The convention is adopted here of using 'Fascism', with a capital 'F', for the Italian example and 'fascism', with a small 'f', for the more general phenomenon.)

In 1938 the German novelist Thomas Mann judged that fascism was 'a disease of the times, which is at home everywhere and from which no country is free'. Many political commentators agreed with him. Fascism was, quite simply, 'the plague of the twentieth century'.[1] There seemed to be fascist movements in virtually every European country. In Italy *Il Duce,* Benito Mussolini, had come to power in 1922, a year which he soon decided should begin an entirely new calendar: it would be Year One in the Fascist Era. In Germany the *Führer,* Adolf Hitler, had come to power in 1933, proclaiming the inauguration of a Thousand Year Reich. Over the next few years other states - including Spain and Austria - seemed to fall prey to fascism, and Hitler's aggressive foreign policy looked likely to herald fascist domination of the whole of Europe, and perhaps of the world. A new dark age seemed about to dawn.

The fascists were defeated in the Second World War and their grandiose designs came to nought; but fascism is of profound historical significance. Indeed it is one of the most important themes in modern history, as well as one of the most fascinating and disturbing. Yet it is also one of the most daunting and least studied. Students often shy away from looking at the general theme of fascism, preferring instead to look at individual regimes, especially Italy and Germany. By focusing on one country only, however, we miss the chance to compare regimes, to understand the links between them and to see them in perspective.

There are several reasons for this unwillingness to study what is often called *generic* fascism - i.e. fascism that is European and possibly worldwide, and not confined to a single country. It is worth being aware of half a dozen such reasons (and of their inadequacy):

i) It is, of course, easier to focus on a single country. There is, quite simply, less work to do. (But a historian cannot avoid hard work.)

ii) The relevant time-scale is uncertain. When did fascism begin? There is no easy answer to this question, since the roots of fascism can be traced further and further back into the past. Similarly, when did fascism come to an end? Many believe that it has not yet done so, and some pessimists believe that it will be increasingly important in the years to come. (These problems do make the study of fascism difficult. Yet they apply to the study of many other historical issues, like nationalism for instance.)

iii) The relevant geographical span is also uncertain. Was fascism confined to Europe, or did it exist outside Europe, for instance in Japan, South America, South Africa, etc? (Once more, historians cannot shirk difficulties - otherwise we'd shirk history entirely.)

iv) Some of the books on generic fascism - and especially those on the theory of fascism - are virtually unreadable. They are full of abstruse philosophical terms and of impenetrable sociological jargon: it is almost as though they are written in a foreign language. Many have tried to read the standard works on fascist theory - and many have fallen asleep or cursed the authors for writing in such a tortuous style. (This is a much more valid reason for sticking to a single-country approach! Nevertheless, no self-respecting history student should ignore the role of ideas in history. After all, they may be absolutely vital. Therefore we must at least grapple with them; and if many of the books on fascism are abominably written, we must seek for those which pay their readers the courtesy of defining the technical words used.)

iv) Fascism deals with aspects of reality - like brutality, murder and even genocide - which we find abhorrent or distressing. We want to condemn it, not analyse or seek to explain it. Similarly, fascism built on irrational emotions which, perhaps, are not amenable to rational analysis. (This is indeed a problem, and one which makes the study of fascism especially difficult. Yet it also applies to the study of single regimes. In addition, it is precisely because fascism was wantonly destructive and barbaric - and may be again - that we must seek to understand it. To do this, we have to use all our powers of reason; and, in addition, we must use our emotions to try, however imperfectly, to enter into the minds of the fascists, their supporters and their victims.)

v) Fascism is very difficult to define. In particular, it is extremely hard to distinguish fascist from other right-wing movements. To decide which party or regime was fascist and which was merely conservative, even if of an authoritarian variety, is a real problem. Very few groups called themselves 'fascist'; the word was more commonly employed by their opponents, who used it loosely. George Orwell, for instance, judged in 1944 that, for most people, 'fascist' was synonymous with 'bully'.[2] In short, the term has been used too often and too imprecisely, so that it has degenerated into a mere term of abuse. Nowadays the term 'fascist' signifies disapproval but otherwise conveys little meaning. (Again, this is no excuse for failure to tackle the issue. After all, almost all political 'labels' are used somewhat laxly, so that their meanings are stretched and become hazy. Words are imperfect instruments of communication, but they are all we have got and we must make the best of them.)

vi) Finally, it must be said that historians are in fundamental disagreement about fascism. Some use the term in a general (or 'weak') sense to refer to all authoritarian groups, providing they were not communist; others use it in a much more closely-defined, specific (or 'hard') sense, which applies to fewer groups. Some have in mind Mussolini's Italy as the model for fascism, while others see Hitler's Germany as the archetypal fascist state. In fact there is no generally accepted definition of the term, and nor is there consensus about exactly which political parties or regimes qualify as fascist. These two issues, of course, are part of a common problem: unless we know what fascism was (or is), we cannot decide which regimes should be classified as fascist; but unless we know which were the fascist regimes, how can we possibly define the characteristics which unite them as fascist? A vigorous debate has taken place among historians, political scientists and philosophers on these issues, and several competing definitions of generic fascism exist. To compound the problems, however, some historians deny that there was any such thing as generic fascism. According to their viewpoint, there were authoritarian regimes and parties in Europe, certainly, but it makes no sense to apply the word 'fascist' to them: they were separate and, moreover, significantly different. The only regime which should be termed fascist, according to this interpretation, was the original self-styled Fascist regime of Mussolini. In short, the differences between the so-called fascist regimes outweighed the similarities, and therefore it makes no sense to employ a term which obscures this fact. Historians who adopt this viewpoint call Hitler's Germany a Nazi, not a fascist state, and see Fascism and Nazism as fundamentally different doctrines. Similarly, they argue that Franco's regime in Spain was neither fascist nor nazi: it may have borrowed some ideas and techniques from elsewhere, but it was, essentially, itself. It was unique, or, to use a Latin phrase, *sui generis* ('of its own type'). So, indeed, were all the regimes which have been unfairly lumped together under the term 'fascism'. According to this interpretation, therefore, the problem of interwar fascism is basically one of mistaken identify. (This historiographical diversity is one of the major reasons why people shy away from studying generic fascism. The difficulties are indeed profound. Yet such is the disagreement among historians that students of history surely must consider the issues seriously. How can we possibly begin to understand the history of interwar Europe unless we grapple with the issue of whether there was such a phenomenon as generic fascism?)

'Fascism' has, quite rightly, been called 'the great conundrum for students of the twentieth century'.[3] The aim of this book is not to solve the problem - or, rather, the whole series of problems - which fascism poses. It will not provide any ready-made answers. Instead, its aims are more modest. It seeks to introduce and explore the theme of fascism, and to present the range of views which the experts have formulated. Above all, it seeks to encourage students to grapple with the issues and to think for themselves. If its readers are made more aware of the fundamental problems involved in the study of fascism and yet, at the same time, become more willing to confront and tackle them, then it will have succeeded in its purpose. It will be doubly successful if students are encouraged to tackle some of the larger and more complex volumes recommended in the Further Reading section.

1 The Fundamental Questions

Generic fascism is a vitally important area of study. It is also a very diverse one, about which there is fundamental disagreement among historians. To avoid adding to the confusion, therefore, the questions about fascism which are to be explored in the rest of this book must be formulated as clearly and precisely as possible.

a) Why did so many fascist parties and regimes exist in the interwar period?

We must investigate why so many groups which either called themselves, or have been called, fascist appeared between the wars. Were there common, European-wide causes for their growth? Or did fascism spread, like a disease, from one country to another? If either of these interpretations can be proven, then there are good reasons for supposing that generic fascism existed. Or were there particular, and therefore separate, causes operating in different countries? If so, we may decide that notions of generic fascism are faulty.

b) Exactly which regimes should be called fascist?

This is another important, and interrelated, issue. What do regimes need to have in common - in terms of ideas, policies, style, class support, etc - before they can be called fascist? Similarly, how many differences can regimes have before the term fascist should be disallowed? In particular, were Italian Fascism and German Nazism variants of the same movement? And what about other regimes, including Franco in Spain, Salazar in Portugal and Dollfuss in Austria? Do their similarities outweigh their differences?

c) Was fascism a political ideology?

Here we must focus on the ideas associated with fascism. What were these ideas, and do they add up to an ideology (which by definition must be a relatively coherent set of political ideas)? Many anti-fascists have denied hotly that fascism built upon any respectable ideas: they see it as a product of mindless violence or of a peculiar - even deranged - form of personality. Perhaps they are right, but we must not assume that they are. We have, initially, to give fascism the benefit of the doubt and investigate its ideological content. What were its intellectual roots? Did the different fascist movements - or, we should say, the movements which have sometimes been called fascist, and which we may or may not in the end accept as such - have some sort of 'common ideological denominator' or 'minimum'? In other words, are particular ideas necessary components of any movement to be called fascist? Or is fascism a looser ideology than this, so that it includes a broad range of beliefs, no single one of which must be present?

d) Was fascism a 'style' of rule?

Some play down the ideas associated with fascism and stress instead its characteristic forms of political control - its propaganda, its paramilitary organisation, its symbols, rallies and mass mobilisation. To some writers, fascism was fundamentally a style of rule. Indeed some have insisted that it was little more than style - that there was no substance behind the facade. Others, however, insist it was both a style and an ideology.

e) Was fascism the tool of capitalism?

One significant approach to fascism is to focus on its supporters. The orthodox communist approach has been to insist that fascism was a weapon in the class struggle: it was the bourgeoisie's attempt to keep the proletariat in its place and so to prevent revolution. Not only were the mass of supporters overwhelmingly of a single class, the middle class, but - so the argument runs - fascist movements were financed by wealthy capitalists. As a consequence, the seemingly all-powerful fascist dictators were little more than the puppets of their wealthy backers, following policies favourable to them. This is a fertile area for debate. What is the connection between fascism and capitalism? Who were the fascist supporters, members of a single class or of all classes; and did wealthy capitalists control the dictators in any sense?

f) Was fascism similar to communism?

It is instructive to compare fascist states with the USSR. Many have judged that fascism was at the extreme right of the traditional political spectrum: hence it is identified with capitalism and is seen as the complete opposite of communism, which is on the far left. Others have insisted that fascism was a 'third way', being neither capitalist nor communist: instead, fascist thinkers favoured a corporate (or corporative) state, in which the economy was managed by a tripartite alliance between owners, union representatives and government. However, some writers have claimed that, despite surface differences, fascism and Soviet communism were really very similar, both being totalitarian (a type of political system in which the government controls all aspects of individuals' lives). Despite ideological differences, both were dictatorships and both used similar techniques, of propaganda and terror, to control their citizens.

g) What was the nature of fascist regimes?

Once fascists were in power, what did they accomplish? Were they reactionary or were they modernising? What techniques of control did they establish, and how were the people organised? What were the characteristics of the fascist state? How was the economy affected? Did fascists all follow aggressive foreign policies? Did they all persecute minorities?

h) How is fascism best defined?

This is the most fundamental question; and a range of definitions - both simple and complex - will be considered. Some define fascism as a political ideology, while others see it as an ideologically-free - or opportunistic - technique of political control. A third group denies that there was any such thing as generic fascism, seeing it, largely, as the product of historians' loose thinking. In fact, this is the question that most people ask first, but we must reserve our conclusions on this issue, keeping an open mind for as long as possible. In a sense, the answer to it will be the sum total of the smaller, more manageable sub-divisions in (a)-(g).

2 Fascism: a General Outline

a) Italian Fascism and other fascisms

It is sometimes said that the word Fascism derives from the Latin word *Fasces*, which denotes bundles of rods, often attached to an axe, carried in front of the lictors (magistrates of high status) in ancient Rome as symbols of authority, unity and justice. Any meaning deriving from this must be vague, but in fact this was merely an adopted association. Once he was in power Mussolini wanted his regime to be seen as the heir to the Roman Empire, and so he adopted this dignified symbol. In reality, Fascism derived from the Italian word *Fascio* (plural *fasci*), meaning a group, club or band. It was a term associated with rebels. In Sicily in the 1890s, for instance, Fasci of left-wing workers in the sulphur mines organised strikes and demonstrations against the island's wealthy absentee landlords. Yet it is also associated with those right-wing nationalist groups which were in favour of war in 1915 and afterwards, when local Fasci, or patriotic committees, were formed; and after the war nationalists set up their own Fasci, or paramilitary organisations, to combat the left. When, in 1919, therefore, Mussolini formed the *Fasci di Combattimento,* the 'Combat Group', everyone recognised that this was a dynamic, subversive organisation.

Literally, therefore, fascism means something like 'group-ism'. In short, it is not a term which, linguistically, means anything very precise. Perhaps, having been used previously by left and right, it was meant to symbolise the need to transcend such divisions in a new national unity; but this notion is probably a rationalisation after the event, as was the adoption of the lictors' *Fasces.*

Certainly Mussolini did not use the word in any very precise way. In 1919 he insisted that precise ideologies were for intellectuals only:

> We allow ourselves the luxury of being aristocrats and democrats: conservatives and progressives; reactionaries and revolutionaries; legalitarians and illegalitarians, according to the circumstances of the time.[4]

Mussolini had a left-wing programme, calling for the abolition of private property, but a few years later he moved to the right. Clearly he was not bothered about consistency in his ideas. Indeed he was, at different times, monarchist and republican, Catholic and anti-clerical, revolutionary and reactionary, militaristic and libertarian, racist and race-free. Fascism, he insisted, was a 'synthesis of every negation and every affirmation'.[5] In view of his inconsistencies, it is not surprising that many have called Fascism a method of gaining power and thereafter a style of rule, and not a set of doctrines at all. 'Our doctrine is action,' said Mussolini.[6] Perhaps, therefore, his Fascism is synonymous with power politics rather than with any theories. Action comes first, and then the flexible theory of Fascism could be used to justify it - whatever it was. According to this viewpoint, Fascism is no more than a rationalisation of whatever the leader decided, thus making it a 'chaos of contradictions'.[7] In other words, Fascism (Italian style) was power politics and unprincipled opportunism.

Many writers, while not denying some intellectual content to generic fascism, nevertheless insist that it was not a proper ideology. They argue that it lacks intellectual rigour, that it has no agreed intellectual prophets and that its origins are imprecise. In short, fascism was, in Hugh Trevor-Roper's phrase, 'an ill-assorted hodge-podge of ideas'.[8]

Other experts, however, believe that it was an ideology. They have traced its origins back to the Enlightenment of the eighteenth century, and to an intellectual revolt not only against rationalism but against the liberalism, industrialisation and urbanisation of the nineteenth century. Its formative ideas included the notion that life was a perpetual struggle, between nations as well as individuals, that race was a key concept and that each nation had a special identity. According to this interpretation, the forerunners of the fascists existed in the years before 1914, though fascism emerged fully only after the First World War. The mass conflict of 1914-18 boosted fascist ideas and produced a group of ex-servicemen who found it very difficult to reintegrate into normal civilian life. Furthermore, the war destabilised the existing regimes and, more particularly, produced in Russia a revolution by communists dedicated, at least in theory, to fomenting revolution in the West. The fascists gained widespread support by pledging themselves to resist the forces of world communism. In the postwar years a number of movements of fascist type sprang up around the same time, and not only in Italy and Germany but elsewhere too. The key difficulty for the historian is to classify them, resisting the twin temptations of, on the one hand, lumping them all together as fascist and, on the other, of refusing to see any common characteristics because of national differences. Remember that we should expect some differences, if only because the movements, being nationalistic, stressed their separate identities.

b) Preliminary definitions

What were the common ideas associated with fascism? No definitive explanation can be given at this stage, but we can at least state some of the major ideas and alternative explanations.

Almost all writers are agreed that fascists were against liberal democracy and believed in some form of dictatorship. Typically, the fascists also stressed not reason but emotion, and one of their strongest emotions was the insistence on the special identity of nations. They also, in the interwar years, insisted on the importance of the leader, the heroic man of destiny who mystically embodied the nation and had the task of rectifying national wrongs, which could range from territorial to economic grievances. Furthermore, they often stressed struggle and violence.

Can we go further in defining fascism? Many have said that we cannot, insisting that the essence of fascism is not to be found in the realm of ideas. Yet several writers have indeed given fairly short definitions. Here are some examples:

i) Roger Griffin has defined fascism as 'a political ideology whose mythic core in its various permutations is a palingenetic form of populist ultra-nationalism'.[9] This definition obviously needs 'decoding'. First, Griffin is arguing that the central, distinguishing characteristic of fascism is not a matter of fact or logical argument but of myth or energising idea (see page 17). This central idea is of rebirth. ('Palingenetic' means 'expressing the idea of rebirth or of the growth of a new order following a period of perceived decline'.) Fascism was a form of extreme ('ultra') nationalism, motivating and involving large numbers of people ('populist'). Hence fascists called for the creation - or recreation - of a new, more vital nation; and hence, according to this view, fascism is an optimistic, revolutionary doctrine, an important sub-division of nationalism.

Several brief comments must be made. First, there is the implication that fascism can exist without a dominant leader. Some would doubt this. Similarly, there is no mention of racism in general or anti-Semitism in particular, nor of any aggressive, imperialistic foreign policy, or of any particular form of economic organisation. Again, other writers would argue that these are, in fact, the key ideas in fascism. But Griffin is not saying that particular forms of fascism cannot have a strong leader or racist or imperialistic policies, only that they need not exhibit these qualities. It should also be noted that he is not describing any particular regime: he is describing an 'ideal type' or 'model'. He therefore leaves room for significant differences between different fascist states, providing they agree on his version of the core (or lowest common denominator) of fascism. But, once again, some writers would disagree. While Griffin argues that both Fascist Italy and Nazi Germany were fascist states, though with substantial differences between them, some historians say that since the differences between the two states were profound - and certainly in their racial policies they were so - then lumping them both together as fascist hinders our understanding of historical reality.

ii) Roger Eatwell has given us a similar, but significantly different, definition. He calls fascism an ideology 'which preaches the need for social rebirth in order to forge a holistic-national radical Third Way'.[10] Again there is the emphasis on rebirth or resurgence, but he stresses explicitly the radicalism of fascism, the nature of its nationalism and its economic purpose. He uses the word 'holistic' to describe the fascists' idea of the nation: this means 'whole', so that, in some mysterious way, the whole is greater than the sum of the parts, the nation in fact giving meaning to the individuals within it. On the other hand, it should be noted that not everyone would qualify as a member of the nation. In Italy, for instance, the nation included only those who shared the Italian culture, while in Germany those perceived to be of an inferior race could not become true Germans. As for the phrase 'Third Way', this expresses the notion that fascism was neither capitalist nor communist: the corporate state was the fascist alternative.

Eatwell's view overlaps with Griffin's, but he has picked out several alternative features. Even so, his interpretation is open to some of the same objections. He also may give too much attention to ideas, which others will judge to be little more than propaganda. In particular, it may be said that the Third Way was never more than a rationalisation. After all, the corporate state never came about (see page 71).

iii) Another brief definition has been provided by the Israeli historian Zeev Sternhell, who argues that fascism equals 'nationalism + socialism'. This is a commendably brief formulation - or, perhaps, deceptively brief. In fact, the precise meanings of the two ingredients need to be 'unpacked'. By 'nationalism' he means the aggressive, extreme nationalism which became popular at the end of the nineteenth century, and by 'socialism' he means the extreme, Sorelian variety, given to violence (see page 18), not the Marxist type with its emphasis on equality. Sternhell does not stress the importance of leadership or of race, and indeed he insists that Nazism's stress on anti-Semitism and race disqualifies it as a form of fascism. Hence, while fascism equals nationalism plus socialism, National Socialism was not fascist.

iv) A more inclusive view has been given by Ernst Nolte. He argues that a movement qualifies as fascist if it meets a six-point check-list. True fascists must be anti-Marxist, anti-liberal and anti-conservative; and in addition they must accept the 'leadership principle' (i.e. total obedience to a single heroic leader), they must have a party army and they must aim at totalitarianism. Almost everyone has condemned the abstruse way in which Nolte has expressed his ideas, but many - though not all - have agreed with him on the essentially negative character of fascism's aims; and his stress on the organisation of fascism, via a strong leader and a paramilitary organisation, is also instructive. The aim of totalitarianism, imprecise though this is, is also worth considering. Yet many insist that Mussolini never tried to control all aspects of Italian life. Hence Fascism was not fascist.

v) Finally, the most inclusive definition of all has been provided by the American historian Stanley Payne.[11] He insists that fascism can only be understood on three different levels: ideology (and here he draws particular attention to authoritarianism, to the need to create an integrated economic structure and to the goal of empire); the fascist negations (anti-liberalism, anti-conservatism and anti-communism); and style and organisation (with charismatic leadership, the political mobilisation of the masses, the extensive use of political symbols and the exaltation of youth). Yet some have argued that this approach is at once too specific (so that the point about anti-communism does not seem relevant to today's post-communist world) and too general (in that he is trying to pack everything in.) Such an all-inclusive 'check-list' approach might seem calculated to make almost all right-wing movements and regimes seem fascist, but in fact Payne rejects several, including Franco's in Spain.

c) Assessment

There are almost as many definitions, or interpretations, of fascism as there are historians who have studied the issue. Therefore students are advised to be cautious in accepting any of them. After all, historians often have an axe to grind, if only because they look at fascism from the perspective of their speciality. Historians of ideas, for instance, give priority to fascism as an ideology; economic historians stress the vital importance of the way the economy was mobilised in fascist states; and political historians are likely to start off with the preconception that the key issue is power, not the cloudy rhetoric that accompanied or disguised it. On the other hand, we should also - at this stage - be cautious about rejecting any interpretations.

Clearly we must put off reaching final conclusions. Instead, we should try to study the fascist movements - or what are called fascist movements - as open-mindedly as possible, assessing the evidence as fully and impartially as we can before reaching any verdict. In doing so, we should note the common features of these groups but should not ignore what divided them. And if what divided the fascist groups led, in reality, to important differences in action, then the concept of generic fascism may be considered redundant. For instance, the differences over race within Fascist and Nazi philosophy may seem minor, and both can be contained within suitably nimble definitions about 'holistic' nationalism; but in view of the effects of these differences we may nevertheless decide that Fascist Italy and Nazi Germany were very different regimes.

We may end up agreeing with any of the five writers whose views are sketched above, or with none of them. Perhaps we will accept the views of the sceptics, like Denis Mack Smith, who argue that generic fascism is a myth. Perhaps, indeed, all broad theoretical explanations of history must be inadequate since historical phenomena are always more vast and complex than any theory. And yet if every theory is inadequate, some theories are more inadequate than others. In the next chapters, we must measure the theories against our knowledge of the facts and, most important of all, we must seek to understand what happened.

References

1 Richard Bessel (ed), *Fascist Italy and Nazi Germany* (Cambridge University Press, 1996), p. 1.

2 The Collected *Essays, Journalism and Letters of George Orwell*, vol. 3 (Penguin, 1970), p. 138.

3 R.A.H. Robinson, *Fascism in Europe, 1919-1945* (Historical Association, 1981), p. 1.

4 Ibid.
5 Denis Mack Smith, *Mussolini* (Granada, 1983), p. 160.
6 Martin Kitchen, *Fascism* (Macmillan, 1976), p. 28.
7 Mack Smith, *Mussolini*, p. 160.
8 S.J. Woolf (ed), *European Fascism* (Weidenfeld and Nicolson, 1968), p. 20.
9 Roger Griffin, *The Nature of Fascism* (Routledge, 1991), p. 44.
10 Roger Eatwell, *Fascism: A History* (Chatto & Windus, 1995), p. 11.
11 For the views of Sternhell and Payne, see the Further Reading section.

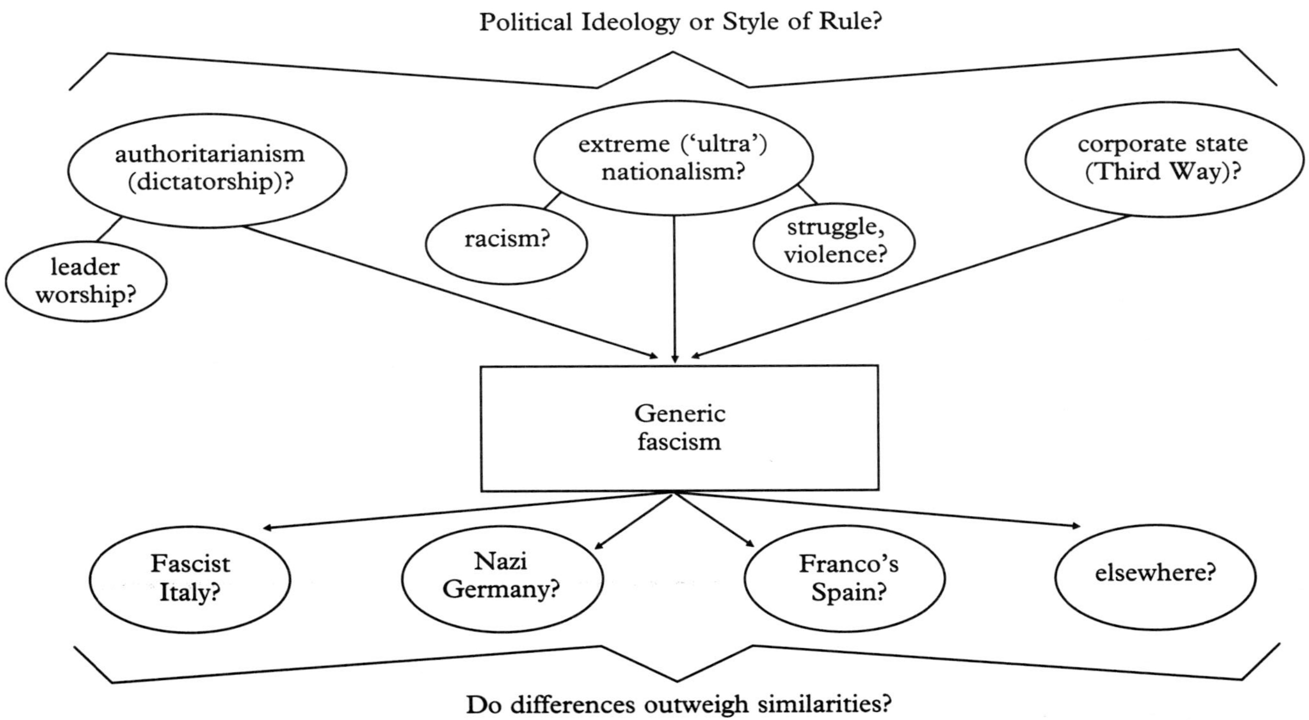

Summary - The Problem of Fascism

CHAPTER 2

The Origins of Fascism

Heroic leaders - or, rather, leaders who were portrayed as heroic by propaganda - were central to the fascist movements and regimes of interwar Europe, and it is often said that the *Führerprinzip* or 'leadership principle' (uncritical acceptance of the leader's policies and decisions) is one of the central tenets of fascism. We must not, however, make the mistake of equating Fascism and Nazism with Mussolini and Hitler. Admittedly these individuals were central to the Fascist and Nazi regimes, but the essential ideas associated with fascism pre-dated the dictators.

1 Intellectual Origins

Many people looked back after 1918 and described the prewar years as some sort of golden age, an unchanging idyll of stability and prosperity. Yet there are few things as fallible as human memory. In reality the decades before 1914 saw unparalleled transformation: it was even calculated, at the turn of the century, that there had been greater changes in the last thirty years than in the previous two millennia. This was an era of extensive industrialisation and urbanisation, and there was also a growing acceptance of liberalism. This was the characteristic ideology of the middle classes. It stressed, economically, that governments should stand aside and pursue policies of *laissez-faire:* the people should follow their own economic self-interests, with a minimum of government interference, and in this way - it was believed - the maximum number would prosper. Politically, liberals insisted that governments derived their legitimacy not from God but from the consent of the governed, and therefore citizens - or at least the educated and responsible middle classes - should have a say in electing them. Since, on the whole, living standards were improving, with even the poorest beginning to live longer and to work shorter hours, many approved of the way in which the new middle classes (the industrial elite) were pushing the older landowning, aristocratic classes (the pre-industrial elite) from the centre of politics. Indeed many rejoiced at the triumphs of industrialisation and looked forward to a future of prosperity and of ever greater middle-class political domination. It seemed to them that progress was almost a law of history.

On the other hand, there were some who were appalled at the changes Europe was undergoing. These included people on the left, the socialists and communists. To their way of thinking, the middle classes were exploiters. Liberalism's stress on individual effort and on an unregulated economy served the interests only of the owners of the means of production, and hence some form of collectivism was needed to help the proletariat. The workers were powerless as individuals, but their solidarity - in trade unions or left-wing parties - could bring enormous gains. There were, in addition, people on the right of the political spectrum who were dissatisfied, though socialist doctrines of class warfare had little attraction for them. These included the pre-industrial elite (monarchs, landowners, clergy and army officers), whose accustomed wealth and power were declining, and members of the lower middle classes - such as small businessmen, shopkeepers and skilled artisans - who were sinking in the social hierarchy because of competition from large capitalist enterprises. Rationalising their grievances, many began to think that modern life was unnatural, unhealthy and decadent. It is also possible that some were becoming bored with the security and general stuffiness of urban life. They wanted excitement and an end to the tedium of routine. Some of these people supported traditional right-wing groups, clustered round surviving monarchies. Others, forming what may be called a 'new right', saw the need for fresh forms of political action, buttressed by new ideologies. It is often said that it was this pre-1914 generation which helped to generate fascism. In particular the 1890s have been called the 'incubatory period of fascism'.[1]

a) The New Right

It is widely accepted that the fascist brew of ideas was being blended before 1914. Its main ingredient was dissatisfaction. Philosophically, there was an attack on many of the most important ideas in European thought since the Enlightenment of the eighteenth century.

The Enlightenment had marked a new confidence in human reason, stressing the importance of rational thought rather than of passive acceptance of authority, tradition or 'the will of God'. Hence it encouraged the scientific view that human beings can understand and ultimately master the world. It therefore stressed material, rather than spiritual, reality. In short, it placed man rather than God at the centre of affairs, being 'homocentric' rather than 'theocentric'; and by the nineteenth century it was associated with industrialisation and liberalism. This new outlook on life was called Positivism (the idea that knowledge and understanding stem from observation and scientific investigation).

Yet there was a backlash. Some disliked the new emphasis on individualism, which bred competition and threatened to destroy not only notions of community but also the sense that there was a transcendent meaning (a meaning beyond the here and now) to life. These people favoured an anti-positivist approach and they were the ideological enemies of capitalism and liberalism. Thus they had something in common with the romantic movement of the eighteenth century, which exalted nature, creative genius and intuition. Romantic philosophers, like Jean-Jacques Rousseau, gave primacy to passion and instinct over mere rational calculation, which was seen as sterile and mechanical. This philosophical outlook was resurrected in the nineteenth century by thinkers like Henri Bergson, who insisted that instinct (*'élan vital'*) was more important than mere intellect. Vitalism (belief in a creative life-force dwarfing reason) thus challenged Positivism. In addition, nineteenth-century thinkers of the new right tended to look back nostalgically to a pre-industrial way of life. They called for radical changes which would produce a new society and yet, at the same time, contrive also to return to past traditions. In particular they believed in the nation, which Rousseau had defined, lyrically and mystically, as 'the dead, the living and the yet unborn'.

Undoubtedly members of the new right tended to be nationalistic. In this respect they were not the opponents but the heirs of the Enlightenment. The eighteenth-century philosophers had stressed that governments derived their authority from the people and that, therefore, the people could change state boundaries. By the nineteenth century this had led to the widespread view that distinct groups of people, united by language or other factors, formed 'cultural nations'; and each of these - each *Volk*, to use the German term - should, if necessary, be allowed to redraw political boundaries in order to occupy its own nation state. Hence dynastic empires should be broken down into their component peoples. Liberal and new-right thinkers had this view in common. What distinguished the nationalist ideas of the anti-positivist minority was their extremism. Such was their abhorrence of individualism that they exalted the nation to a supreme place, so that it almost seemed as though individuals had value only as part of a larger whole. In their view, man was created for the nation, not the nation for man. Such extreme ('ultra') nationalism went beyond reason: instead, it was a passionate faith which gave meaning to individuals' lives. Nationalism was a positive commitment of the new right, as it was later to the fascists - showing that fascism was not solely a negative, 'anti-ideology'.

2 The Ingredients of Proto-Fascism

Most historians are agreed that fully-fledged fascism did not exist before 1914. After all, no one even used the term then. Nevertheless, we can see that many of the ingredients of the later fascist movements were coming together. In other words, fascism existed in a rudimentary, unfinished form. Hence it is often called proto-fascism ('proto' meaning a first, unfinished version).

We have distinguished several strands in the thinking of the right. There was anti-positivism and anti-materialism, together with hostility towards capitalism, industrialisation, urbanisation and liberalism. There was also hostility to the socialist idea of class warfare. On the more positive side, there was a belief in the value of human instinct and emotion and a commitment to extreme nationalism. Furthermore, some were beginning to demand a new form of economic organisation. Capitalism pitted owner against worker; but some members of the new right argued that owners and workers should come together in corporations and organise industry for the benefit of all. In this way, competition within the state would be eliminated, and there would be a return to the co-operation which was supposed to have existed in the medieval guilds. According to theorists of what later became known as the corporate state, this form of economic organisation would promote national unity, not class division. Here was another positive proto-fascist idea.

For greater clarity about the nature of proto-fascism, we need to study the impact of several important nineteenth-century thinkers who, unwittingly, contributed to the fascist matrix. No more than a few are covered here, but it should be recognised that there were many. Indeed the origins of proto-fascism encompassed not only intellectual theories but also developments in the arts, where there was a romantic revival. The composer Wagner, for instance, created a mystical German past inhabited by exalted heroes.

a) Sorel and Syndicalism

Georges Sorel (1847-1922) was a French socialist philosopher. Disgusted with the increasing moderation and reformism of so many European socialists, whom he believed to be collaborating with the capitalist enemy, he argued that socialism could only be achieved by a general strike to overthrow the whole system. He urged workers to form revolutionary trade unions, or *syndicals,* and take direct action. After their success, there would no longer be a government or 'state' (the repressive apparatus by which one class ruled over another): instead there would be anarchy, which he defined as the spontaneous co-operation of individuals; and therefore his ideas are sometimes called Anarcho-Syndicalism. As a non-Marxist socialist, his thinking was far more acceptable than Marx's to many right-wingers; but it was another aspect of his thinking which was to prove most influential to fascism, that of political 'myths'.

Sorel believed that what really motivated people was not dispassionate analysis but emotion and, especially, myth - by which he meant an idea, not necessarily logical or true, which has the power to move men to action. Such a myth, for instance, was the second coming of Christ to the early Christians. And such was the idea of the general strike to socialists:

> Strikes have engendered in the proletariat the noblest, deepest and most moving sentiments that they possess: the general strike groups them all in a co-ordinated picture, and, by bringing them together, gives to each one of them its maximum of intensity; appealing to their painful memories of particular conflicts, it

> colours with an intense life all the details of the composition presented to consciousness. We thus obtain that intuition of Socialism which language cannot give us with perfect clearness - and we obtain it as a whole, perceived instantaneously.[2]

There was thus something mythic (or 'mystical', not 'mythical' or false) about the idea of a general strike, and it was this inspiring conception - rather than the reality of a strike, which was likely to be all too prosaic - which Sorel stressed. He thus saw the vital importance of ideas which could energise and inspire individuals. He also knew that these myths could be especially powerful when associated with violence, which by its very nature tended to arouse the emotions and temporarily shut down the logical mind. The premise of such reasoning, therefore, was that human beings are only partly logical: it is the emotions which provided the mainspring of action, a view with which many contemporaries agreed. Gustave Le Bon, for instance, in his *The Psychology of Crowds* (1895), judged that the credulous masses were swayed more by charismatic leaders than by reason. The great Austrian psychologist Sigmund Freud was also arguing in the years before 1914 that man was dominated by irrational instinctive drives (in the id, or unconscious mind) which the conscious, rational mind (or ego) could scarcely comprehend, let alone control.

Such reasoning probably had more effect on the political right than the left, and most commentators believe that Sorel contributed to the construction of fascism. Indeed Roger Griffin (see page 9) believes that a 'mythic core' lies at its centre. The central myth to fascists was the nation.

b) Social Darwinism and Nietzsche

In the 1890s and after many people accepted the view that life was an unending struggle in which only the fittest survived. The idea derived from the evolutionary theories of Charles Darwin (1809-82), who believed that species survived by adapting to cope with the rigours of the environment. In fact Darwin's ideas were put forward tentatively; but his followers, beginning with Herbert Spencer, produced a highly simplified version of Darwinism and applied it to human societies. According to this Social Darwinism, nations were like animals and all had to struggle and fight in order to survive: those who won would grow stronger and flourish, while those who lost would decline and fall. What nations could not do was to live in peace with each other: the only alternatives were to progress or regress. In short, nation eats nation, just as dog eats dog. These views were of profound importance around the turn of the century, and most historians believe they influenced fascism. After all, Hitler's autobiography was called *Mein Kampf* ('My Struggle'), and the Führer once insisted that the stark choice in life was to be either 'hammer or anvil': one was either struck or did the striking.

Ideas like these affected social attitudes before the First World War. They can be seen, for instance, in the cult of manliness that affected educational practice. They also led to a glorification of war. Furthermore, they affected individual thinkers, perhaps the most influential of whom was the German philosopher Friedrich Nietzsche (1844-1900), a man often identified as one of the philosophical founders of fascism. In fact, Nietzsche is a figure very difficult to pigeonhole. In some respects he seems a typical product of the late-nineteenth century, reacting against the rationality of the Enlightenment. He was an anti-positivist who insisted that ideas were to be judged not by their truthfulness but by their usefulness: what mattered was not whether a notion corresponded to any abstract truth but whether it was creative or inspiring. He exalted healthy human instincts above mere rationality, and was thus a Vitalist. He was also a homocentric thinker, coining the phrase 'God is dead', and a Darwinist, believing that evolution had not come to an end and that man could be replaced by the Superman. Finally, he was seeking for a transcendent purpose to his life, over and above mere pleasure, which he dubbed 'miserable ease'. Yet if his thinking was in some ways typical, it was also very unusual.

An extract from his best-selling book *Thus Spoke Zarathustra* (1888) is instructive:

> You should love peace as a means to new wars. And the short peace more than the long. I do not exhort you to work but to battle. I do not exhort you to peace, but to victory. May your work be a battle, may your peace be a victory! You say it is a good cause that hallows even war? I tell you: it is the good war that hallows every cause. ...
>
> 'What is good?' you ask. To be brave is good. Let the little girls say: 'To be good is to be what is pretty and at the same time touching' ...
>
> Let your love towards life be love towards your highest hope: and let your highest hope be the highest idea of life! ...
>
> 'This is now my way: where is yours?' Thus I answered those who asked me 'the way'. For THE way does not exist.
>
> 'Why so hard?' the charcoal once said to the diamond; 'for are we not close relations?'
>
> Why so soft? O my brothers, thus I ask you: for are you not my brothers?
>
> Why so soft, so unresisting and yielding? Why is there so much denial and abnegation in your hearts? So little fate in your glances? And if you will not be fates, if you will not be inexorable: how can

> you - conquer with me?
>
> And if your hardness will not flash and cut to pieces: how can you one day - create with me?
>
> For creators are hard. And it must seem bliss to press your hand upon millennia as upon wax, bliss to write upon the will of millennia as upon metal - harder than metal, nobler than metal. Only the noblest is perfectly hard ...[3]

These words seem to be glorifying war and the soldier's bravery. As Nietzsche put it on another occasion, we should 'live dangerously'. Mercy and tenderness are perceived as vices, and the military qualities of courage and endurance as virtues. Hardness - suggesting strength, determination and resilience - was also a virtue, and Nietzsche seems to be urging everyone to cultivate this quality: we all have in ourselves the potential for heroism, even if we seem weak. After all, what is charcoal but a form of carbon - as is diamond, the hardest of all substances? The method for transforming weakness into strength, he often insisted, was to develop one's will-power. The writing is also highly emotive. Like poetry, it has the capacity to affect the emotions. But also like poetry, the passage is hard to pin down to a single meaning. In fact, Nietzsche was not a political creature at all, and he once said that the militarisation of Germany in the 1870s and 1880s was 'the destruction of the true German spirit'. When he spoke of waging war, he probably meant metaphorically, not literally: one should wage war on one's own follies and self-deceptions. He was an individualist, and as such he was not prescribing any course of action for other human beings. How could he? God did not exist, he believed, and therefore there could be no prescribed - or God-given - purpose in life. There were not even any set moral values. We all have to choose our values and our purposes. Hence *the way* - the way we should all follow, laid down by some authority - does not exist.

Nietzsche did influence the fascists. Many of them mimicked his style of writing (often producing exalted and rapturous nonsense to inflame the spirit). They, like he, often emphasised will-power, and sometimes they spoke of the Superman. Mussolini, in public, seemed almost the embodiment of the machismo (or aggressive virility and masculine pride) which Nietzsche seemed to praise. Yet it is unfair to call Nietzsche a prophet of fascism. Some might argue that his insistence that there are no God-given values opened the flood-gates for fascist atrocities; but many others were saying much the same thing around this time, and it should not be forgotten that Nietzsche influenced humanitarian thinkers, like the writer Hermann Hesse. Most important of all, Nietzsche argued again and again against the mindless obedience of human beings to any authority. Nietzsche, the prophet of individualism, would surely have had complete contempt for the regimentation that existed in fascist regimes.

c) Racism and the Racists

A belief in the racial superiority of whites, and the inferiority of non-whites, was extremely common among Europeans in the nineteenth century. The Scottish anatomist Robert Knox began his book *The Races of Man* (1850) with the assertion that 'race is everything', and thirty years later Disraeli added in a novel that race was 'the key of history'.[4] It seemed that everything - except the differences between individuals of the same race, about which a discreet silence was maintained - could be explained by these means. Character and temperament, ability and culture, the past and the future - all were determined by race. Scientists believed that just as there was a hierarchy in the animal kingdom, with man at the top, so there was a hierarchy among the races of mankind. The lighter the colour of the skin, so ran their simplistic message, the higher the race on the evolutionary scale; and only palefaces - like the scientists themselves - could be truly civilised.

Notable publications in this pseudo-scientific field included Arthur de Gobineau's *On the Inequality of the Human Races* (1852), a book whose title well indicates its content. He believed that human history was largely the product of the natural antagonism which existed between the races. Another important work was *The Foundations of the Nineteenth Century* (1899) by Houston Stewart Chamberlain. This was a broad survey of European culture which stressed the importance of racial purity. Chamberlain saw European history as largely a struggle between Germans (the Aryan inheritors of Graeco-Roman civilisation) and the Jews (the enemies of mankind). Hitler, who was greatly influenced by the book, was to be profoundly moved on meeting Chamberlain at Bayreuth in 1923, paying tribute to his wisdom in *Mein Kampf*.

Increasingly, as the nineteenth century wore on, there began to be a racial component to anti-Semitism. Hostility towards the Jews was no new phenomenon: indeed it was age-old. The Jews, who had been barred from landowning and government service in many European countries, were virtually forced into business, as well as the professions, and were widely scapegoated as usurers and exploiters. But in the past anti-Semitism had generally been rationalised with religious arguments, especially the charge that the Jews had killed Christ, whereas now it was increasingly being justified on racial grounds. The apparently scientific nature of such prejudice made it all the more respectable. The Jews were presented as a unique race, and a subversive and corrupting one. Around 1913 the *Protocols of the Elders of Zion* was published, containing details of an alleged Jewish conspiracy to rule the world. This was another book that greatly influenced Hitler and the Nazis. That this clear forgery was believed in some quarters is an eloquent testimony of the extent, and the irrationality, of anti-Semitism at this time.

3 Proto-Fascists Movements

There were no fully-fledged fascist parties before 1914. Compared to the later movements, fascist organisations were no more than embryonic: hence they were 'proto-fascist' bodies. At least this is the view of many historians. Yet it is emphasised that these groups were often somewhat incoherent: their doctrines were less than clear-cut and their aims had seldom been formulated with clarity. Certainly there existed a new right, but we should resist the temptation to lump all such groups as proto-fascists. The more moderate and traditional opponents of modern life - for instance the pre-industrial elite - are best called conservatives, and rather than adopting any Nietzschean or Vitalist new philosophy they continued to draw their inspiration from Christianity, which they interpreted as requiring submission to the civil authority ('Render unto Caesar the things that are Caesar's'). They also emphasised the importance of tradition and of legal continuity. Nevertheless some members of the pre-industrial elite did see the need to adapt their beliefs. This was especially so of monarchists in countries where the monarchy had been abolished: they were virtually forced to modify their ideas, often calling for a much more authoritarian monarchy than in the past. They also combined the older concept of monarchy with the new notion of nationalism, arguing that a reformed monarchy could, in some mystical way, embody the spirit of a nation. In addition, however, political groupings were formed with a more obviously proto-fascist agenda. Some asserted that human beings - being irrational, potentially violent and yet component parts of a larger national whole - needed strong leadership not democratic chaos.

We should not be dogmatic about exactly which groups should be called proto-fascist. Since fully-developed fascism is a controversial and somewhat indistinct concept, proto-fascism must necessarily be so as well. What is clear, however, is that in several countries those on the political right exhibited new qualities, some of which were later taken up by the fascists in the interwar period.

a) France

The capture of the French Emperor in 1871 meant that the Third French Republic was instigated by default. But defeat by Prussia, and the loss of the provinces of Alsace and Lorraine, produced a sense of aggrieved nationalism which threatened to undermine the new regime. It seemed possible that a monarchy might be restored or that another form of right-wing authoritarianism might come about. In 1882 the League of Patriots was formed, and at the end of the decade a coup in favour of the charismatic General Boulanger seemed possible. At the turn of the century, French society was chaotically divided, as was shown by the celebrated Dreyfus Affair; and the legal wrangle over whether Dreyfus was innocent or guilty of passing military secrets to Germany revealed the existence of widespread anti-Semitism.

In 1899 Action Française was founded. Its economic doctrines were corporatist and its members, as well as attacking the general concepts of parliamentarism and individualism, were clearly anti-Semitic. Not surprisingly, therefore, it has been identified as a proto-fascist body. Nolte sees in it 'the beginnings of fascism'.[5] Certainly its leader, Charles Maurras, put forward ideas which may broadly be classified as proto-fascist. Indignant at France's defeat by Prussia in 1870-71, and at her continued weakness thereafter, he found an explanation in weak, self-seeking bourgeois politicians: there almost seemed to be a conspiracy - by Protestants, freemasons and Jews - to bring about French decline. His cure was national unity, which only a single leader could bring about. Maurras was very influential through his newspaper *Action Française,* and his ideal of the incorruptible leader did have widespread appeal. On the other hand, his real aim was the restoration of the monarchy as the embodiment of French nationalism. Furthermore, Action Française had little mass appeal and made little attempt to secure any. It was a patently elitist organisation, drawing much of its rationale from old-fashioned Catholicism. The cocktail of ideas with which Maurras and Action Française were associated did have something in common with what was later called fascism, but it is safest to conclude that nevertheless they should be distinguished from it.

b) Germany and Austria

Owing partly to nineteenth-century *Völkisch* movements, which stressed the mystical bonds which united members of the nation, nationalism was strong in Germany. Nor did it subside into mere patriotism after Bismarck had brought about unification in 1871. On the contrary, nationalism was still powerful, building on the dissatisfaction that not all German-speakers - especially in Austria - were contained in 'Lesser Germany'. Economic growth, which bred a consciousness of strength, added stridency to calls for the liberation of the fatherland from foreign influences (which were said to include industrialisation and hedonistic materialism) and for the expansion of the empire. Furthermore, both militarism and anti-Semitism were growing towards the end of the century.

Proto-fascism in Germany has been associated with both individuals and groups. The former included Otto Böckel, who won a seat in the Reichstag in 1887 as an independent anti-Semite and soon held rallies and torchlight parades in Marburg, and Paul Botticher, who insisted that Jews were the 'carriers of putrefaction' and 'bacilli ... to be destroyed as quickly and as thoroughly as possible'.[6] In short, the new right insisted that not all German-speakers were truly members of the German *Volk:* nationality was essentially a matter of blood not language. The groups included the Pan-German League and the Navy League, which combined strong anti-Semitism with calls for an aggressive foreign policy. The connection between these ideas and later Nazism is obvious.

Many Germans in the Austro-Hungarian Empire had similar views. Feeling threatened by other national groups, the Germans responded with an extreme form of nationalism and with rabid anti-Semitism. It was in Austria - especially in Vienna before the Great War - that Adolf Hitler imbibed anti-Semitic and other popular prejudices. He also learned a lot from the political parties that existed then, especially Karl Lueger's Christian Social Party. In 1895 this organisation gained control of Vienna, retaining it until 1910, and Lueger was an extremely popular mayor, appealing especially to the lower middle class and to their anti-Semitic prejudices. Yet Lueger was a moderate compared to some. For instance, an unbalanced anti-Semitic ex-monk, Adolf Lanz (1874-1954) - who was obsessed with blonde, blue-eyed womanhood - called for intermarriage with 'inferior breeds' to be prohibited and even advocated the castration and extermination of Jews. From his castle home he flew the swastika flag, an ancient symbol mistakenly believed to be of German origin. He later claimed that Hitler had stolen his ideas

Germans in other parts of the Austro-Hungarian Empire, especially in Bohemia, were even more extreme, and in 1904 the German Workers' Party was formed, identifying Jews, social democrats and big businessmen as the enemy. In the 1920s it helped bring about the formation of the Austrian Nazi party. It should be remembered that it was in Bohemia, at Braunau, that Hitler had been born in 1889.

c) Eastern Europe

Several extreme right-wing parties existed in this area. In Serbia, for instance, there was 'Unification or Death' (otherwise known as the 'Black Hand'). It called for an expansionist foreign policy and for an authoritarian government. Even in Russia a proto-fascist body has been identified: in 1905 the 'Union of the Russian People' was formed, in order to defend the Tsar, the church and the fatherland. It was anti-liberal, anti-Semitic and used violent tactics to break strikes: its paramilitary force, the Yellowshirts, beat up opponents in general and Jews in particular.

d) Italy

Proto-fascism grew in Italy as a reaction to the perceived failure of the new Italian state, which had been formed in the 1860s but which did not bring about the progress and modernisation for which many had hoped. There were also complaints that pockets of Italians lived under foreign rule and that the country was doing poorly in the scramble for colonies.

Particularly humiliating was the defeat of 20,000 Italians at Adowa in 1896 at the hands of King Menelik and his Abyssinian tribesmen, the only major reverse suffered by a European power during the partition of Africa.

On an individual level, there are several thinkers whose influence has often been seen as preparing the way for interwar Fascism. Certainly there was a definite anti-positivist revolt in Italy, and nationalism and syndicalism began to grow into important forces. Giovanni Papini, from Florence, wrote in 1912 that violence, rather than parliamentary hot air, would spell salvation for the nation: 'The future needs blood. It needs human victims, butchery'. He added, two years later, that Italy was a country of 'botched attempts' ruled by 'the old, the incapable, the charlatans'. His aim and that of like-minded followers was, he insisted, to 'take off our jacket, roll up our sleeves and see whether this old Italian shit can finally be turned into a fine stone statue'.[7] The programme of the Futurists, an artistic avant-garde group founded by Filippo Marinetti in 1909, expressed similar views, emphasising violence, conflict, nationalism and imperialism.

The most important proto-fascist body in Italy was the ANI (*Associazione Naziolalista Italiana* - the Italian Nationalist Association), founded in 1910 by Enrico Corradini and others in order to encourage the government to conquer Libya, whose Arab inhabitants they dismissed as wild beasts who should be whipped. The connections between this body and the later Fascists are unmistakable (and in 1923 all its members were to join Mussolini's Fascists). It adopted the economic ideas of Professor Alfredo Rocco, who was calling for an authoritarian corporate state, in which representatives of the unions and the owners would be regulated by politicians. Yet it is easy to exaggerate the influence of the ANI before the war. The party was small and confined largely to intellectuals, and even when Italy did make war on Libya there was little mass enthusiasm. Certainly the socialists were against the conflict, one of the leading lights in the socialist party - Benito Mussolin - insisting that 'To us the national flag is a rag to be planted on a dunghill'.[8] Nor was there any anti-Semitism, an absence which distinguished the Italian new right from that in most other European countries. In Italy there were only about 50,000 Jews, approximately 0.1 per cent of the population.

4 Assessment

The last decades of the nineteenth century saw a revolt against science, rationalism, individualism and materialism. The prevailing liberal political economy seemed to some to produce selfishness, unwelcome class divisions, urban poverty and general decadence. This anti-positivist reaction took several forms. Some people turned to essentially apolitical activities: there was a vogue for occultism, for instance, while many took up rambling or organised sports. But the main backlash was political: and it even seemed that the extreme left and the extreme right might be united in their joint opposition to liberalism

a) Nationalism and Socialism

The relationship between the adherents of nationalism and socialism was in fact complex. On the one hand, they had aims and policies in common. After all, both were collectivists, being enemies of individualism and of the unregulated economy, and as a result they often pursued similar policies. As mayor of Vienna, for instance, Karl Lueger carried out the same sorts of reforms which, enacted by left-wingers in Britain, were called municipal socialism. Indeed some nationalists did proclaim themselves socialists, Corradini, the founder of the ANI, even speaking of 'national socialism' and hoping to win the support of Italian workers. Another common feature was the undemocratic spirit of groups of their members. Nevertheless, there was hostility between them. One divisive factor was their contrasting views on equality, those on the right being far more likely to insist that human beings were essentially unequal. But the key issue was their attitude to class and nation. Most people on the left believed in class allegiance irrespective of nationality, working men of all countries having nothing to lose but their chains: socialism was therefore an internationalist doctrine, stressing the brotherhood of all working men. Most right-wingers, however, judged that the members of a nation belonged to an organic (living) community which rendered class divisions unimportant. They considered socialism a cure worse than the original disease, involving not just class division, which was bad, but actual class war, which was far worse. In general, therefore, nationalists opposed the socialists, and *vice versa.* While socialists called for a revolution against the exploitative middle classes, the nationalists pinned their hopes on a national revival to end crass materialism and produce a more dynamic form of political organisation.

b) Was Proto-Fascism a reality?

Fascism - or, rather, proto-fascism at this time - rested squarely on nationalism and authoritarianism. Yet identifying proto-fascism, let alone defining it, is extremely difficult. All proto-fascists were nationalists, for instance, but not all nationalists were proto-fascists. Similarly, all proto-fascists were authoritarian, but not all those who favoured some form of authoritarianism were proto-fascists. A similar formulation may be used of race. Many proto-fascists were racists, but not all racists were proto-fascists. Nor should all syndicalists be called fascists, far from it, though the proto-fascist right did take some ideas from the syndicalist left. Furthermore, it is not easy to distinguish between those large numbers, best called conservatives, who opposed many of the trends in modern life, and the smaller numbers who were such rabid opponents that they deserve to be called forerunners of fascism. Separating the two is made the more difficult in that both groups, anti-liberals all, had similar enemies and so were allies of convenience.

We must also recognise that proto-fascism was a vague set of ideas. This is, in fact, only to be expected. Given the uncertainties and controversies that surround the fully-fledged concept of interwar fascism, how could an unfinished version be expected to exhibit any real clarity? Furthermore, proto-fascism was eclectic, drawing its inspiration from many and diverse sources, some of which - like the writings of Darwin or Nietzsche - were interpreted in ways their authors did not originally intend. There were also different combinations of these constituent elements in different countries.

To the question 'Did proto-fascism amount to an ideology?', sceptics may answer No. There are several reasons for this, over and above the difficulties of identifying which bodies deserve to have the term applied to them. Above all, an ideology must - by definition - exhibit ideas which fit together into a relatively coherent whole. Yet while some proto-fascists wanted the formation of a new society, others wanted the resurrection of an old one, and a third group managed to call for both at the same time. Proto-fascism, stressing the bonds that unite members of the same nation, is often seen as a revolt against individualism, and yet some were attracted to the new right as a possible antidote to the dull, featureless uniformity which they feared in liberal democracy.

Sceptics may argue that proto-fascism was in reality remarkably incoherent and that, therefore, the term has no value. Yet if proto-fascism was part of an anti-positivist revolt, that is a revolt against rationality, should we not expect it to exhibit logical inconsistencies? After all, what matters from the fascist perspective is strength of feeling not rational consistency. Furthermore, it can be argued that proto-fascism was indeed more coherent than fascism after 1918, when dictators like Mussolini and Hitler exalted the leadership principle to a new prominence. At least before 1914 proto-fascists did not all insist on mindless adherence to the whims of an all-powerful leader.

At any rate it is possible to discern 'fascist-like ideas' - a deliberately loose phrase - in the decades before 1914. These ideas include the notion that violence was important, and not only as a means to an end but as an end in itself. The viewpoint is well expressed by the poet W.B. Yeats, in his poem from 1938 'Under Ben Bulben':

1 Know that when all words are said
And a man is fighting mad,
Something drops from eyes long blind,
He completes his partial mind,

For an instant stands at ease,
Laughs aloud, his heart at peace.
Even the wisest man grows tense
With some sort of violence
Before he can accomplish fate,
Know his work or choose his mate.

These words, like Nietzsche's, also give us some understanding of the appeal of fascism, which, at its most idealistic, seemed an heroic attempt to transform human life into something higher. Calling for a more abundant life, fascism appealed to noble self-sacrifice, to youthful idealism and romanticism - though, of course, the practice was sadly different from the theory. Do Yeats's words not also, as a statement from 1938, show the similarity between prewar and postwar thinking? We can often see connections between fascist statements from before and after 1914. Indeed it is this similarity which lends credence to the proto-fascist strands which historians have discerned before the war.

Consider the following statements, all from interwar fascists, which exhibit characteristics of pre-1914 thinking.

i) Sir Oswald Mosley, the British fascist leader, writing in *The Greater Britain* in 1932:

> We ask those who join us to march with us in a great and hazardous adventure. We ask them to be prepared to sacrifice all, but to do so for no small and unworthy ends. We ask them to dedicate their lives to building in this country a movement of the modern age. … We ask them to re-write the greatest pages of British history by finding for the spirit of their age its highest mission in these islands. … Those who march with us will certainly face abuse, misunderstanding, bitter animosity, and possibly the ferocity of struggle and of danger. In return, we can only offer to them the deep belief that they are fighting that a great land may live.[9]

ii) Dean Denis, describing the Belgian fascist party, Rex:

> Rex is not an adventure. It is something much more beautiful than an adventure. This great departure, this moving break with the past, this fantastic enterprise likely to attract spirits enamoured of the absolute, is an answer to the call that comes from far in the past, from far in the present.[10]

iii) The leader of the Portuguese fascist National Syndicalists, Rolao Preto, calling for change in 1934:

> A terrible wave of utilitarianism and baseness is sweeping through

the world, and is threatening to subvert and vulgarize everything, plunging it into a quagmire of tragic moral degradation. ... The clear and holy light of ideas is covered up and lost sight of under a cheap blanket of unfettered commercialism which darkens the soul. ... But there are independent spirits, free spirits, those who are prepared to embark on a hard road of sacrifice to preserve their pride and the glory which their independence and freedom give them. They should not despair. Already the signs of reaction are becoming manifest in the noisy protest on every side from those able to resist the temptation to trade their own dignity for material comforts, to swap strength of character for the possibility of making money. ... The Revolution is under way. It will redeem man, raising him to the height of all the divine greatness that is his.[11]

iv) In Romania Codreanu laid down rules for the fascist Iron Guard:

Be disciplined, for only thus will you win through. ... Work every day. Put your heart in your work. Let the reward of your work be not gain but the satisfaction that you have done your share to advance the Legion and improve Romania. ... Speak when you need. Your oratory is the oratory of the deed. You act; let others talk. ... Fight and never be a coward. Leave the ways of infamy to others. It is better to fall fighting with honour than to win through in infamy.[12]

v) Alfred Rosenberg, one of Hitler's earliest mentors and the semi-official philosopher of National Socialism, in the 1920s:

History and vocation no longer consist in [the] struggle of class against class, church dogma against church dogma, but in the struggle between blood and blood, race and race, people and people. And this means: values of soul fight against values of soul. That history must be judged from the point of view of race is a truth which will soon be self-evident. ... But the values of the soul of race, which are the motive powers behind the new philosophy, are not yet part of actual general knowledge. Now soul means race from within. Conversely, race is the outside of a soul. To call to life the soul of race is to recognize its supreme value and, under its guidance, to give the other values their organic position: in state, religion, and in art. This is the task of our century: to create a new type of man out of a new myth of life.[13]

These are all, to some degree, incantations rather than reasoned political arguments. They exhibit definite emotional qualities and have therefore been dubbed 'adolescent' by university professors. (It should, however, be noted that such characteristics can appeal to people of all ages: certainly quite a few professors in the interwar period were not immune.) Yet it must be conceded that fascism seemed to offer something above selfishness. In addition, we can see a similarity between these extracts and writings from the prewar period (for instance, from Sorel, Nietzsche and Papini). In short, fascism did not spring into being fully formed in the 1920s, and there are definitely connections between pre-1914 and post-1918 ideas. We may well conclude that interwar fascism could not have existed without its 'incubatory period'. Nevertheless, it was still not fully formed by 1914. Certainly it had relatively few supporters. It first needed the impetus of the crisis that engulfed Europe from 1914 to 1918.

5 The Impact of the First World War

Contemporaries believed that the war which broke out in July 1914 would be a glorious adventure: it would, in a British phrase, be 'all over by Christmas'. How wrong they were. It turned out to be an inglorious war of attrition which dragged on until November 1918 and resulted in approximately nine million deaths.

Some historians have argued that the war changed everything, creating a new world. Such a view is exaggerated. There were continuities between prewar and postwar life which have too often been overlooked. Certainly liberal democracy continued to flourish in several countries, like Britain and the United States. Yet it must be admitted that the war changed much. Warfare itself became mechanised and more destructive, as developments in science and technology were applied to weaponry. There were important economic consequences as well, including much devastation, and a significant number of men in the prime of life were either killed or maimed. Government spending rocketed during the war, causing inflation, and afterwards the cost of war pensions added to the burden of repaying wartime loans. It seemed, in the aftermath of war, that Europe's economic prosperity had been destroyed for at least a generation. Furthermore, political upheaval accompanied economic instability. There were even problems in the neutral states of Spain and Portugal, and when Portugal did join the war in 1917 there was a short-lived dictatorship. Greece's entry saw the overthrow of its monarch. Moreover the war led to the overthrow of Europe's dynastic empires. The Romanovs were toppled in Russia in 1917, and the German Hohenzollerns and the Austrian Habsburgs fell as the war was lost. It was hoped that democratic regimes would take their places, and optimists believed that the break-up of the Austro-Hungarian Empire into its component 'cultural nations', each occupying its own nation state, would take the sting out of nationalism and remove a prime cause of war.

In fact, nationalist groups were far from satisfied. When peace treaties were drawn up, in Paris after the war, it was found impossible to satisfy all their demands. It is true to say that after the peace treaties, and the consequent redrawing of boundaries, fewer people felt that they were living under alien rule. But it was not possible to satisfy all the people. The geo-political map in 1918 was too complicated and confused for that. To put it simply, the different 'cultural nations' did not all occupy separate pieces of land which they could claim as their state. In addition, it was decided that the new states had to be 'viable', large enough to be likely to survive economically and militarily. The result was that most of the new states contained significant minorities. Problems were being stored up for the future, especially since many such minorities were German.

It was agreed at Paris that Germany had been responsible for causing the war. Hence no one advocated allowing the Germans national self-determination, especially since a 'Greater Germany' would surely dominate the whole continent. But the punishment meted out seemed anything but just to most Germans, and so German nationalism, already boosted by the war, was further inflamed. The same was true of other countries. The war had stimulated nationalist feeling, and where a country lost the war, or - as with Italy - was perceived to lose the peace, such emotions continued to run dangerously high. The extreme 'ultra-nationalist' ideas of the new right thus became more acceptable to more people. Furthermore, the war had important psychological effects. The actual combatants were militarised, so that it was hard for them to reintegrate into normal civilian life. After the trauma of the Western Front, men could not simply pick themselves up, brush themselves off and start all over again. Nor were the majority, the non-combatants, unaffected: after the meaningless slaughter on the western front, it was hard for them to assume any longer that all was right with the world. Many began to doubt that progress was a law of history. Instead, there was increased fear and insecurity.

The communist revolution of 1917 was also a tremendous shock to many in Europe. While some applauded, hoping that the rest of Europe would follow a similar path, others felt dangerously menaced. If the revolutionary left was about to come to power, should not anti-communists support the groups on the extreme right which promised fierce resistance? Nolte has argued that the origin of fascism lay always in the challenge of communism. Many on the right took to the streets to face the challenge. There can be little doubt that, in the shadows of the Great War, a significantly new context had been created - with political, economic, social and cultural components - favourable to the growth of fascism.

References

1 S.J. Woolf (ed), *European Fascism* (Weidenfeld and Nicolson, 1968), p. 27.
2 David Smith, *Left and Right in Twentieth-Century Europe* (Longman, 1970), p. 81.

3 Friedrich Nietzsche, *Thus Spoke Zarathustra* (Penguin edition, 1961), pp. 74-5, 213, 231.
4 George Watson, *The English Ideology* (Penguin, 1973), pp. 204-5.
5 Ernst Nolte, *Three Faces of Fascism* (Weidenfeld and Nicholson, 1966), p. 25.
6 F.L. Carsten, *The Rise of Fascism* (Batsford, 1967), p. 26.
7 S.G. Payne, *A History of Fascism 1914-45* (UCL Press, 1995), p. 63; Roger Griffin, *Fascism* (OUP, 1995), p. 23.
8 Carsten, *Rise of Fascism*, p. 21.
9 Sir Oswald Mosley, *My Life* (Nelson, 1968), pp. 334-5.
10 Eugen Weber, *Varieties of Fascism* (Van Nostrand, 1964), p. 37.
11 Griffin, *Fascism*, p. 193.
12 Weber, *Varieties of Fascism*, pp. 100-1.
13 Ibid, p. 155

Source-based questions on 'The Origins of Fascism'

1 The statements of five interwar fascists

Read the extracts from the fascists quoted on pages 28-29 and answer the following questions:

a) What did Denis mean by 'spirits enamoured of the absolute' (lines 3-4)? Were similar ideas implicit in any of the other extracts? (4 marks)
b) What similarities are there between the ideas in these statements and those of Nietzsche? Refer to particular passages. (6 marks)
c) Explain what contemporaries may have found appealing about the first four statements. (6 marks)
d) What do you think Rosenberg meant by the 'soul of race' (lines 5 and 10)? How persuasive to you find the phrase? (3 marks)
e) What were the main differences between the messages of the authors? (6 marks)

Hints and Advice: Questions of this type are extremely common in examinations, and hence you must have practice at answering them. The first requisite is a clear understanding of the passages. So read them through slowly several times: after the second reading you should be able to judge the mood of the authors. If you are unsure of this, try reading them to yourself in different 'tones of voice' until you have identified the one which best suits the actual words. The second requisite is to use your knowledge of the general context in order to help interpret the passages. In other words, bring your existing knowledge to bear. Carry out these preliminary activities slowly and carefully, before you start to answer the precise questions set. There is no sense in hurrying, or in trying to write as much as possible. Remember that quality, not quantity, gets the best mark. Always choose your words carefully, and always make sure that you are

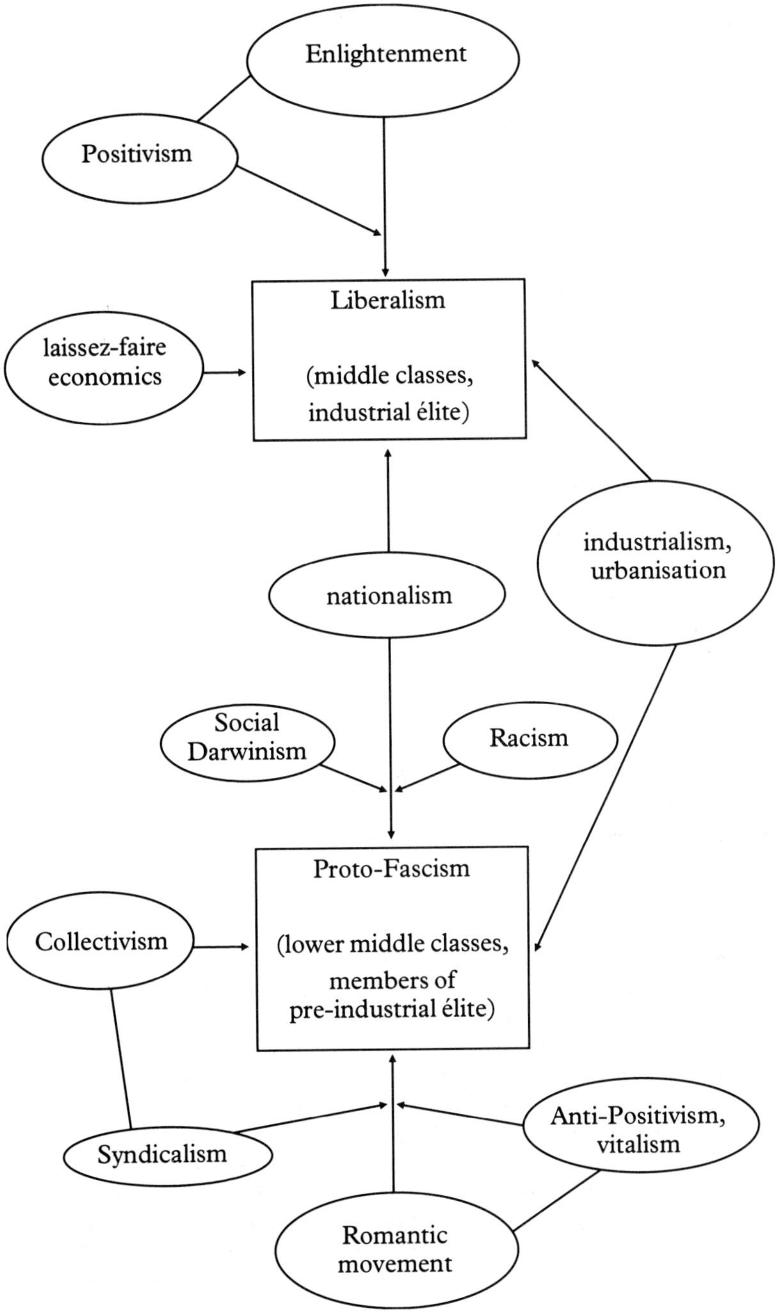

Summary - The Origins of Fascism

answering the precise question set.

a) Consider the possible meanings of the term. Consider also that it may have no precise meaning but simply give - or seem to give - some sort of religious connotation to Rex. Mosley does not use a similar term, but the idea of religious sacrifice is implicit in what he says. Preto's 'free spirits' were also, presumably, enamoured of the absolute. What about Codreanu and Rosenberg? In particular, look at the former's condemnation of the 'infamy' of the opposition, and the latter's words about 'supreme value'.

b) Use this question as an opportunity, first, to show your knowledge of Nietzsche and, more generally, of Social Darwinism. In short, you need to formulate some well-chosen words on the general context. But you must also focus on precise similarities. What will you include, besides the stress on struggle, will-power and heroism? Do the statements emphasise the Nietzschean Superman in any sense? It is also worth pointing out, briefly, that the religious aspects of the statements contradict Nietzsche.

c) Note that the question refers to contemporaries. You do not, therefore, have to say what you find inspiring - unless you explain that fascism appealed to something relatively permanent in human nature. Hence you can once again bring in the general ideological context of the time. In order to generate relevant points, try referring to both particular and general ideas. Also, pay attention to the style in which they are expressed. Note the paradox that while the fascists called for deeds not words, the words are skilful. Did they appeal essentially to the emotions, rather than encouraging logical, sceptical thought? Why would self-sacrifice be appealing, especially if ultimate victory is assured? Would the references to the past be inspiring in any way, in an age of nationalistic fervour?

d) This is a difficult question, but do not dodge it. Your only chance of gaining marks is to address this question, not some other, simpler one. The fact that its meaning is unclear is perhaps the key to the phrase, and to the whole passage. His differentiation between 'soul' and 'race' suggests exact, scientific expertise, but perhaps Rosenberg was trying to blind his readers with science. What significance do you assign to the term 'myth' in the final line?

e) Notice Preto's explicit condemnation of the existing society in his country. But do you think that a similar condemnation is implicit in the need for fundamental change expressed by the other authors? Note also Rosenberg's stress on race. None of the other authors mentions this in the extracts quoted. They may, however, have done so elsewhere in their writings: an acknowledgement to this effect will show examiners that you are aware of the brevity, and thus inadequacy, of all such extracts. What exactly are the authors asking their readers to do? Are some calling for political action and others merely urging the acceptance of a particular viewpoint? If you think there are few differences, say so explicitly.

CHAPTER 3

The Rise of Fascism

1 The Problems of the Postwar World

In 1918 an age of democracy seemed to be dawning in Europe. The old Habsburg monarchy collapsed, and in addition the autocratic Ottoman Empire dissolved. Instead new democratic states appeared, including Austria, Hungary, Czechoslovakia, Poland and Yugoslavia, while Romania and Greece were enlarged and Bulgaria was made smaller (see the map on page 36). Admittedly the Bolsheviks led an undemocratic government in Russia, but this seemed unlikely to last long and at least was no more autocratic than the old Tsarist regime had been. Most important of all, there was a peaceful revolution in Germany. The Kaiser abdicated a few days before the armistice in November 1918 and a new democratic republic was set up. Here was a triumph for liberalism and the positivist spirit. For the first time the nation's government was to be elected by the people. Germany seemed about to take its place as one of Europe's most important democratic states.

Such hopes proved delusory. From the very beginning democrats had enemies - from the far left, looking to communism for inspiration, and from the far right, calling for authoritarian rule. Most people today take the superiority of democracy for granted, but early in the twentieth century democracy had not proved its worth and large numbers preferred undemocratic forms of government.

The age of democracy failed to dawn. Instead there was an age of violence and authoritarian rule. There was, to borrow the title of E.H. Carr's book, a 'Twenty Years' Crisis'. In fact, there were four main interlinking problems, all stemming in part from the war: communism, aggrieved nationalism, economic depression and democratic weakness.

(i) There was conflict between Russia and the rest of Europe. At first the West intervened in the Russian civil war on the side of the anti-communist Whites. Then, after the victory of the Reds, there was ideological tension between the West and the new Union of Soviet Socialist Republics, as the Tsarist Empire was renamed. In effect, a 'cold war' existed, though the term had not yet been coined. The Soviets called for world revolution, urging workers to overthrow their capitalist exploiters, and the Western states responded by treating the USSR as a pariah nation.

(ii) The dissatisfaction of so many Powers with the peace settlement threatened to undermine European stability. Indeed there was a host of grievances throughout Europe which nationalists could try to inflame.

(iii) Major economic misfortune afflicted Europe in the 20 years after the war. There was immediate hardship, with high unemployment and mounting inflation. Next there was a relative boom in 1924-28. Then, from 1929 onwards, the problems became more severe: there was no

Post-war Europe, circa 1937: The Eclipse of Democracy

inflation this time, the prices of goods actually falling, but unemployment reached unprecedented heights. This was a truly wordwide depression, and many began to fear - and the communists to hope - that the whole capitalist system was breaking down.

(iv) The existence of fragile and inexperienced democratic states was another problem, particularly in central and eastern Europe. Could the new states survive, especially since they often contained not only separate 'cultural nations', who disliked each other, but also many smaller minorities? In fact, despite the efforts of the peacemakers, they did not prove to be viable. Carr believes that the division of eastern Europe into small, relatively weak states was a 'dangerous fiasco'[1], creating a virtual vacuum of power which tempted Great Power intervention. But the future of several older states was also in jeopardy, especially when they had a legacy of prewar socio-economic backwardness (as in Spain and Portugal) or where there were few democratic traditions (as in Italy and Germany). Perhaps democracy had been introduced too swiftly, so that its roots never went deep enough.

The result of these issues was that democracy was eclipsed. Yet it survived in several states, including Britain, France and Belgium. Even here, however, undemocratic parties, both communist and fascist, were set up. In Britain, for instance, ex-Labour cabinet minister Oswald Mosley set up the British Union of Fascists (BUF) in 1932, though it failed to attract more than 50,000 members and never looked likely to come to power. In France there were far more fascist-like groups, including Action Française and several leagues of ex-servicemen, the combined membership of which may have exceeded 350,000. Yet despite more street fighting than in Britain, the extreme right failed to break through to power. It was a similar story in Belgium. The key figure here was Léon Degrelle, who devised Rex (from the phrase *Christus Rex* - Christ the King) first as a religious movement, to regenerate Christianity, and then as a political anti-communist league. But in 1939 Rex won a mere four seats out of 202 in the Belgian parliament. Only after the German invasion in 1940 did right-wing groups in France and Belgium, backed by the Nazis, come into their own.

How can we explain the survival of democracy in these states? A basic answer can be formulated by reference to the four postwar problems identified above. The communist threat was not perceived to be momentous enough to provoke a right-wing backlash, though it was certainly much greater in France than Britain; there were far fewer nationalist grievances among these victors of the First World War (especially since France recovered Alsace and Lorraine under the terms of the Treaty of Versailles); the effects of depression were less devastating than elsewhere, and several anti-democratic groups - including the BUF in 1932 and the French Popular Party in 1936 - were formed too late, just as the depression of the 1930s was beginning to lift;

and these were relatively mature democracies and therefore unlikely to collapse. Yet a more comprehensive answer would require other variables to be taken into account, including the political and economic inheritance in each country ('historical factors') and also the actions of important individuals and luck ('contingent factors'). It is such variables which, seemingly against the odds, account for the survival of democracy in the new state of Czechoslovakia.

In other countries it was a different story. In Italy Mussolini set up a dictatorship, and in Germany the Weimar republic gave way to Hitler's authoritarian rule. Democracy also collapsed in Hungary, Austria, Poland, Spain, Portugal and elsewhere.

The relevance of fascism to the four major problems of the postwar era seems obvious enough. Its supporters put forward fascism as the antithesis of communism, and many supported it as the only real alternative to red revolution. Also, there is little doubt that fascism fed on nationalist grievances. It is also apparent that fascism was enormously boosted by economic dislocation: many who supported it did so as a last-ditch remedy for a desperate economic blight. Finally, fascists - or, rather, people who have been called fascists - came to power in Italy and Germany and, at the very least, helped to undermine democracy elsewhere. Indeed many commentators in the interwar years believed that fascism was, quite simply, the next unfolding era of world history.

Nevertheless we must be careful not to assume too much. Given the difficulty of defining fascism and of pinpointing exactly which individuals, parties and regimes were fascist, we must investigate the eclipse of democracy with an open mind, reserving our judgement about the meaning and importance of fascism for as long as possible. The rest of this chapter examines the proliferation of undemocratic parties and states during the 1918-39 period, assessing what they had in common and whether they may be considered part of a single, if multi-faceted, fascist movement.

2 Italy

It was in Italy that the first self-proclaimed Fascist regime came to power. The Italian Fascist leader Benito Mussolini became Prime Minister in October 1922 and set up a dictatorship in 1925-28. In doing so, he created some sort of model for aspiring right-wing parties elsewhere. His success can be explained by two main causes - the weakness of the existing regime and the strengths of the Fascists and other opposition groups. Within both these broad categories, we will see specifically Italian factors (both historical and contingent) and the four general, European-wide problems identified above.

a) Liberal Italy

It was clear in the immediate postwar years that the liberal regime in Italy was unstable. Its weakness can be explained to some extent by historical factors. Italy, unified in the 1860s, was not a united or harmonious state, and the new regime had never achieved much popular support. At first only two per cent of the population were allowed to vote, and politics were the preserve of a small, wealthy elite. In 1912 all this changed: the Prime Minister, Giovanni Giolitti, extended the vote to all men from the age of 30, while all literates, together with those who had completed military service, could vote at 21. Perhaps this would generate enthusiasm for the parliamentary regime, especially since by this time Catholics were no longer forbidden by the papacy from taking part in politics. But, in fact, little changed. Elections simply became more corrupt than ever, and governments proved no more popular or long-lasting. One problem was that liberal Italy had no strong Liberal party or indeed any real party system: instead, there existed a large number of factions clustering around prominent individuals. After an election, deals were done in which the support of opposition politicians was bought by high office. The result was a series of fragile alliances which could only survive so long as divisive issues were avoided. To a growing number of critics, including socialists and syndicalists on the left and nationalists on the right, democratic politics were a corrupt game divorced from the needs of the country.

To historians, looking back on events, it seems that the liberal regime had significant successes. Northern Italy was partially industrialised, for instance; the country took part in the European diplomatic system (joining the Triple Alliance with Germany and Austria-Hungary in 1882); and African colonies were gained (Eritrea and much of Somaliland in the 1890s and Libya in 1912). Yet contemporary critics pointed to the regime's failures, especially to the poverty-stricken, bandit-ridden south of Italy, where so many Italians were illiterate and where communications were so poor. Furthermore, Italy was never considered a Great Power, Bismarck commenting scathingly that she had 'a large appetite but small teeth'. The shameful defeat at Adowa (see page 25) was remembered, not the successes of the scramble for Africa. The root cause of all these problems seemed clear - the weak, corrupt parliamentary system.

The weaknesses of the liberal regime were exacerbated by the First World War. Italy stayed out of the conflict at first but joined in 1915, when the Entente Powers promised territorial gains. Italy backed the winner, but victory came very slowly and her own war effort was anything but glorious. Five million Italians were conscripted and most fought bravely, but their equipment was poor and casualties were heavy (with around half a million killed and the same number maimed). After almost two years' fighting, the army suffered a catastrophic defeat by the

Austrians at Caporetto in November 1917. Italian casualties included 40,000 killed, while 300,000 were captured and many deserted, the rest retreating in disarray for almost 100 miles. It was a tremendous blow to national pride. It is true that revenge came the following year, the Italians taking half a million Austrian prisoners in the battle of Vittorio Veneto and forcing Austria to sue for peace; but by this time Italian discontents had multiplied to dangerous proportions. The very future of the unified state seemed in doubt.

At the end of war the government faced massive problems, including a sense of aggrieved nationalism stemming from diplomatic defeat at the Paris peace conference - or, rather, from perceived defeat. In reality, the Italian delegation did not do badly, gaining the southern Tyrol (called by Italians the Alto Adige), Trentino and Istria, all from Austria-Hungary. As a result, the Italian state now included 200,000 German-speakers (in the Alto Adige) and around half a million Slovenes. Yet the Italians did not, as expected, receive Fiume or Dalmatia, both of which became part of the new Yugoslavian state (see the map on page 36). Nor did they receive any new colonies in Africa. It seemed a 'mutilated peace'. It was also well known that the Allies had treated the Italian delegates without respect. The British attitude at Paris may be judged from the opinion of the head of the Foreign Office that the Italians were 'the most odious colleagues and allies ... "the beggars of Europe" are well known for their whining alternated by truculence'.[2] He, and other foreigners, could not help contrasting unfavourably present-day Italy with the glories of her classical past. What a pathetic decline there had been since the days of the Roman Empire! Many Italians, longing for a return to the greatness of the past, felt the same way.

A sign of the times came in September 1919 when, in defiance of the Versailles settlement, the poet and novelist - and admirer of Nietzsche - Gabrielle D'Annunzio seized Fiume, of mixed Italian and Croat population, with a group of war veterans. Already popular because he had fought in the war, despite being over fifty, and had lost an eye in the conflict, D'Annunzio now became a national hero. He held the port for over a year, and in this time he did much to establish the style of what soon became known as Fascism. He called his men legionnaires, after the soldiers of the Roman Empire; he dressed them in the distinctive black shirts, signifying death, of the crack wartime troops, the *Arditi* ('Daring Ones'); and he instructed them in the Roman salute (with right arm extended) and taught them to sing the *Giovinezza* ('Youth', later the Fascist song). He also delighted in elaborate ceremonials and in general showmanship and was adept at haranguing admiring crowds from the balconies of splendid buildings. Furthermore, he encouraged strong-arm tactics against his enemies, sometimes forcing them to drink a litre of castor oil. To some (but not those on the receiving end), it was all a welcome contrast to the dull drabness of democratic failure.

The state of the economy seemed to rule out any national revival. The war had proved tremendously expensive and had necessitated borrowing on a massive scale. Furthermore, there was inflation and growing unemployment. As a result, soldiers were often unable to get jobs or reintegrate into normal civilian life. To this volatile mix was added another key factor, communism, encouraged by Bolshevik success in Russia and by high unemployment at home. Many peasants in the south began to seize the lands on which they worked, and in the cities of the north workers occupied the factories or went on strike. There was also increasing violence. Many Italians feared a revolution and, at the same time, had lost whatever little faith they ever had in the democratic system.

In 1919 the Catholic Popular Party (PPI) was formed, marking the full participation of Catholics in the political life of Italy. The liberal regime also extended the franchise, so that all adult men could vote, and introduced a system of proportional representation in place of the old first-past-the-post system. Yet no tangible benefits followed. Proportional representation made it even more difficult for any single party to gain a majority in parliament, and most governments were unstable coalitions. Characteristically, there were six different prime ministers from 1919 to 1922.

b) The Fascists

While D'Annunzio was seizing Fiume, the ex-socialist Benito Mussolini, who later borrowed many of his ideas, was little known. Yet, taking heart from the fear of communism that existed and also from the presence of so many returning soldiers, he called for an anti-communist revolution. In 1918 he insisted that soldiers should not stand aside from politics: 'We, the survivors, who have returned, demand the right of governing Italy'.[3] In his view there should not be a democracy but a 'trenchocracy', rule by those - like himself - who had served in the trenches and shed blood for their country. Soon he called this creed Fascism.

Mussolini (1883-1945), the son of a blacksmith and a schoolmistress, had become a leading figure on the revolutionary wing of the Italian Socialist Party (PSI) and editor of its newspaper *Avanti!* before the First World War. At this time he was undoubtedly a socialist, arguing for a minimum wage and for worker participation in management decisions and mocking imperial pretensions, believing that Italian workers should refuse to fight their working-class brothers from other nations. Yet he split with the party in 1914 - over its anti-war policy. Perhaps he believed that large-scale war might hasten a revolution. Certainly he now talked in Sorelian fashion about the need for regenerative violence and about the power of myths to motivate the masses. He campaigned for Italian entry into the war and, with money from the French government and from Italian capitalists, began his own paper, *Il Popolo d'Italia* (note that the title refers, nationalistically, to the whole 'people of Italy' and not, socialistically, just to the working class). The internationalist had become a zealous nationalist. This is not to say that he was anxious to fight. Instead of volunteering, he waited to be conscripted. Nor did he distinguish himself as a soldier, though he later told stories of going over the top and of picking up and throwing back enemy grenades before they could explode. He was invalided out of the army early in 1917 after a grenade-throwing machine blew up during a training exercise. He then resumed the editorship of *Il Popolo,* blaming the government for Italy's poor performance in the war.

After the war Mussolini put himself forward as one of the 'trenchocracy'. He was still a socialist, he insisted, and he wanted collective action to improve working conditions and create a fairer society: but he was also a nationalist, acutely aware of nationalist grievances and violently opposed to doctrines of class warfare. He called himself an 'antimarxist and ... national socialist'.[4] He also wanted to maintain the wartime spirit of self-sacrifice and discipline. In March 1919 he helped to found the *Fasci di Combattimento* (see page 7), whose programme combined left- and right-wing demands. The implication was that the new organisation transcended old-fashioned party or class loyalties. It described itself not as a party but as an anti-party, while its doctrines amounted not to an ideology but to anti-ideological relativism. What mattered was not logical consistency, he insisted, but bold action. His message was aimed above all at ex-servicemen, and several founding Fascist members were from among the *Arditi.* Sceptics, however, decided that Mussolini was merely an opportunist, tempering his ideas to suit the needs of the day and wishing to appeal to as many people as possible - and having no scruples about making contradictory promises.

Only about a hundred people had attended the launch of this 'Combat Group' in Milan. Other ex-servicemen's associations were attracting more support, and in the elections in November 1919 the *Fasci* did not win a single seat, Mussolini himself polling less than two per cent of votes in Milan. Socialists took pleasure in carrying past his home a coffin inscribed with his name. The organisation well might have faded away had not the socialists (the PSI) won one-third of the votes in the 1919 general election, becoming the largest single party (with 156 seats out of 508); and they did even better in the local elections of the following year. The socialists' rhetoric spoke of violent revolution, and a wave of strikes hit town and countryside: 1919 and 1920 were the *Biennio rosso,* the 'two red years'. Many right-wingers feared a left-wing revolution, and yet the government was adopting a policy of non-intervention, reasoning that workers were less dangerous in the factories than on the streets. Hence the official policy was to wait for the strikes to burn themselves out or even to urge employers to give way. It was therefore up to right-wing capitalists to take the initiative themselves

- and in Mussolini, who now shrewdly denied any socialist beliefs, they found a willing accomplice. His followers, unscrupulous and unrestrained in their tactics, became preeminent among large numbers of paramilitary forces. Fascist squads, each of around 40 men led by an ex-officer, successfully broke strikes and destroyed socialist trade unions and town councils, often with the connivance of the local authorities. The result was that the Combat Group - wearing a paramilitary uniform of black shirts and giving the one-arm salute which D'Annunzio had made popular in Fiume - was given a new lease of life. Membership grew from about 20,000 to almost 200,000 in the first six months of 1921.

Yet there were several problems with Mussolini's tactics. First, left-wing supporters might be alienated. More important, Mussolini might lose control. The initiative often passed to local bosses, the *Ras*, including powerful men like Roberto Farinacci in Cremona (whose university thesis had been copied word for word from someone else's) and Italo Balbo in Ferrara; and indeed it was they, by their exploitation of local antagonisms and rivalries, who were producing much of Fascism's success. Indeed it probably makes more sense to think in terms of several provincial Fascisms at this time, rather than of one unified movement.

It was at this stage that the politicians intervened. The ageing Giolitti, the supreme political manipulator of the prewar years, offered an electoral alliance to Mussolini, believing that the Fascists could be tamed by entry into the system. Mussolini gladly accepted: continued violence might lose the support of the right-wing capitalists, and so it was time for another tactic. In the elections of May 1921 the Fascists won 35 seats and Mussolini himself was elected. Another important change came in October 1921, when the Fascists ceased to be a mere 'Group' and became instead a political party, the National Fascist Party (PNF), with a right-wing programme. Mussolini's motives are not hard to fathom: not only would the Fascists now have a new political respectability, but a party, with prescribed rules, would be easier to control than an unwieldy movement. In addition, the jettisoning of left-wing views would smooth his relationship with his capitalist backers. Yet the *Ras* were unhappy with these tactics. Wanting to end the existing system, not participate in it, they indulged in more and more violence. Mussolini managed to convince the liberals that he and he alone could restrain them and calm the situation. But could he?

Matters came to a head in 1922. The *Ras* became more open in their challenge to the state authorities: Philip Morgan has called this 'a kind of creeping insurrection'.[5] Mussolini feared decisive retaliatory action from the government; but, luckily for him, the reaction came instead from the left. In July the socialists organised a general strike, to coerce the government into taking action against Fascist violence. Their tactics proved a complete failure, and the strike was compared to the rout at Caporetto. Not only did it last for a mere two days, but the Fascists took firm action against the left, Mussolini posing as the defender of law and order. Fascist terror was imposed on much of Italy, and yet many on the right condoned this action and considered the Fascists indispensable. Then Mussolini, perhaps pushed by his followers, decided to act. He let it be known in October that he was organising a March on Rome, which would amount to a violent seizure of power. This was the last straw for many politicians, who decided to ban the Fascists. Then, at the last minute, Victor Emmanuel III refused to declare martial law and, rebuffed, the government resigned. The king's motives are uncertain. Perhaps he was influenced by his mother, who was an ardent Fascist supporter. Perhaps he had no confidence in the liberal politicians. Probably he simply wanted to avoid civil war. At all events, Mussolini was invited to join the government: refusing to accept any other office, he was made Prime Minister on 31 October 1922. At 39 he was the youngest premier in Italian history.

Mussolini had achieved the premiership constitutionally. There was no armed insurrection. Soon the Fascists boasted that they had seized power, and that 3,000 of their number had been martyred in the process; but this was patently untrue. The Fascists were murderers, not martyrs. Rather than marching on Rome, Mussolini arrived in the capital by train and went to see the king wearing a bowler hat.

c) The Dictatorship

Technically the liberal regime was not over. Mussolini was not a dictator: in his fourteen-man cabinet there were only four Fascists, and furthermore his supporters were a small minority in the parliament. Yet its days were numbered. Indeed it is hard to avoid the conclusion that the liberals had virtually abdicated. By this time few politicians had any real faith in democracy. Mussolini's first speech as Prime Minister was a vicious attack on parliamentary democracy, but he received a vote of confidence and was given powers to make laws without parliamentary consent for 12 months. Five former prime ministers voted in his favour. Few Italians could avoid drawing a contrast between liberalism, which seemed old and impotent, and Fascism, which seemed young and virile. Liberalism was thus dead - or perhaps it had never been fully alive.

We cannot be sure what Mussolini's precise aims were, especially since the movement contained those who wanted consolidation and those who wanted radical change. But he certainly intended to increase his power, and this he did in several ways. Press censorship began, and there was a reign of terror, as thousands of political opponents were arrested and many were beaten up or killed. The Fascist Militia was set up in 1923, a private army paid for by national taxes. Mussolini undoubtedly wanted to eliminate opposition, but he realised it could not by done immediately: he said he would pull out one tooth at a time, so that people would not realise what was happening. As well as violence, therefore, he also used conciliation. Certainly he got on better terms with the papacy, increasing the pay of the clergy and introducing religious instruction in schools and universities. He also declared swearing illegal and banned obscene publications and the distribution of contraceptives. Constitutionally, he introduced the Acerbo law, specifying that the party receiving the largest number of votes, providing they totalled a quarter of all votes cast, would take two-thirds of the seats. The measure received a parliamentary majority, though only in an atmosphere of intimidation: the chamber was surrounded by armed Blackshirts. Mussolini was preparing the ground for the 1924 general election. Even so, he left nothing to chance, and the elections were marked by widespread corruption, intimidation and violence. A British journalist judged that 'the fascists are, in their methods, as barbarous as the bolsheviks: for the moment, at any rate, foreigners cannot regard Italy as a civilized country'.[6] Hundreds were killed and wounded, and the socialist leader Matteotti was tortured. In the end, the Fascists and their allies received 65 per cent of the vote and had a clear majority in the chamber.

Matteotti's efforts to have the election results declared invalid led to his murder on 10 June 1924, by Amerigo Dumini and other Fascist thugs. (Dumini had once slapped a girl for wearing a red carnation, and,

Cartoon of Mussolini sitting on Matteotti's coffin

when her mother and brother protested, he shot them dead.) Mussolini protested his own innocence of the crime, and indeed he had probably not authorised it; but, almost certainly, he had let it be known that he wanted rid of this turbulent socialist. There followed a storm of disapproval, and public opinion seemed to be swinging against him. Giolitti and other politicians stayed loyal, thinking - fatuously - that this time they could control him, and neither the Pope nor the king turned against him. But socialists and some Catholics and liberals withdrew from the parliament, in a new 'Aventine secession'. Many of the *Ras* were also critical, thinking that Mussolini had sold out to big business. The regime began to totter. Many thought he could not survive, and rumours of his resignation were celebrated in the streets. The cartoon above illustrates the new light in which Mussolini was viewed. There was no caption, but none was needed: the sheer ugliness of the caricature leaves no doubt as to Mussolini's moral character, while his position, squarely on top of Matteotti's coffin, shows his determination not to reveal the truth.

Decisive action was needed in this crisis. Realising that he had to become a dictator or fall, Mussolini established a dictatorship. Opponents were killed or intimidated, and foreign journalists were beaten up or bribed. Soon, following failed assassination attempts, he banned opposition parties, trade unions and strikes. In addition, a secret police, the OVRA, was set up to repress anti-Fascist activity, and Fascist officials replaced elected mayors in local government bodies. By 1928 Italy had become a one-party state.

d) Assessment

Many factors - including the four identified at the start of this chapter - were involved in Mussolini's rise to power after the First World War. Communism was clearly important. Admittedly the challenge from the left seemed greater than it actually was: after all, the communists split from the socialists in 1921, weakening the influence of the left, while many of the strikes were short-lived and ineffectual. Italian car production increased from 34,000 in 1919 to 49,000 in 1920 - not a sign of a country on the verge of collapse. But, even so, it is hard to envisage Mussolini's success without it. Similarly important was the sense of aggrieved nationalism in Italy, which Mussolini insisted he alone could redress. Thirdly, the economic problems of the Italian state were of major importance. Not only were inflation and unemployment problems in themselves, but they exacerbated Italians' perception of the communist threat and even of territorial injustices. Finally, all of these issues emphasised the fourth factor, the weaknesses of democracy in Italy. The liberal regime virtually collapsed in the early 1920s, handing power to Mussolini on a plate. Clearly democracy had not put down deep roots in Italy; and it is even doubtful whether a large number of

Italian liberals should be called democrats at all.

These four factors did not suddenly spring into existence in 1918-22: they were to some extent 'historical' problems, having existed before 1914 and been made worse by the First World War. The war had exacerbated current problems, revealed the inadequacy of the existing regime and created a host of new grievances. Furthermore the war produced a large number of ex-soldiers who were ready recruits for new paramilitary organisations. They were the agents of Fascism. Yet all of the above factors cannot fully explain the rise of Fascism in Italy. We must also consider 'contingent factors' - including luck, chance and unpredictable events. Into this category come the disastrous decision of the left to call a general strike in 1922, the refusal of the king to authorise martial law in the same year and the unpredictable reaction to Matteotti's murder in 1924.

Yet it is often said that good politicians make their own luck, and we must not leave out of account another contingent factor, Mussolini's personal actions. He was an excellent, rabble-rousing journalist and showed considerable skill and courage after the war, not least in imposing leadership on the rather amorphous Fascist party, which built upon regional grievances and could well have collapsed through internal wrangles. He also used violence with extreme ruthlessness, while at the same time insisting that he and he alone could impose law and order. His movement was thus Janus-faced, symbolised by the rubber truncheon (*manganello*) and the double-breasted waistcoat (*doppio petto*). His doctrine of 'Fascism' was also remarkably skilful. It was a very broad, flexible set of ideas, which could appeal to people in virtually every sector of the political spectrum. The essence of his philosophy was not ideological profundity or consistency but the need for action. In some ways, therefore, Fascism was power politics writ large, with power coming from the barrel of a gun. Aside from this, Fascism was a style: it brought panache to politics, motivating the masses and symbolising a welcome and refreshing dynamism.

How far were these factors specifically Italian and how far European-wide? Of course everything that happened in Italy was, in a sense, unique. No two events, or individuals, are ever exactly the same. But are there significant similarities between what happened in Italy and what happened in other areas of Europe from 1918 onwards? We must ask whether a similar set of problems existed in other countries affected by the First World War, and then we must determine whether they followed a similar political path, perhaps evolving similar doctrines and styles. If they did, then 'generic fascism' (see page 1) should be considered an acceptable term. Mussolini chose 'Fascism' because of its peculiarly Italian connotations and at first insisted that it was not for export; but he soon changed his mind and began to think of himself as head of a European movement. But was he being realistic or indulging in wishful thinking? Did fascists come to power elsewhere in Europe?

3 The Military Dictatorships

a) Hungary

The end of war saw social and political incoherence in many areas of Europe, and nowhere was the confusion greater than in Hungary. Formerly a self-governing region of the Habsburg Empire, with 17 million inhabitants, half of whom were Magyars, Hungary now lost half her land and population. Rich landlords held most of the power, but the constitution of the new state took the form of a limited monarchy, with a regent as head of state until a monarch could ascend the throne. Charles IV, the previous Habsburg Emperor, might have become king but for international disapproval. Instead there was violent instability and uncertainty. In 1919 a communist regime was set up in Budapest by Béla Kun, who had joined the Bolsheviks after being taken prisoner by the Russians in the war. It lasted only five months and was crushed by Admiral Horthy, former commander of the Austro-Hungarian navy, who was aided by foreign troops. A reaction then set in, signalled by the appointment of Horthy as regent in 1920.

The Admiral set up a right-wing and fiercely nationalistic regime, building on resentments at the Versailles settlement, and also an anti-bolshevik one. It might seem therefore that he came to power for many of the reasons which affected Italy around the same time. Yet very few - either at the time or later - have used the term 'fascist' to describe the regime. Perhaps this is because, buttressed by the church and looking to Catholicism for ideological support, it seems essentially conservative rather than fascist. Perhaps it is because it exhibited anti-Semitism, unlike Mussolini's Italy. It may be due to Horthy's maintenance of parliamentary elections as a front, camouflaging the undemocratic nature of the regime from outsiders. It should also be recognised that Horthy had few positive policies to boast about, nor - unlike the Fascists later - a propaganda machine capable of manufacturing them. Yet also, perhaps, Horthy's regime is not linked to fascism because, in 1919-20, the concept of fascism was little known in Europe. Had his rule begun a few years later it might now be interpreted differently.

What is generally accepted as the fascist challenge in Hungary came after Horthy had assumed control. Gyula Gömbös, who had spoken of Hungarian national socialism as early as 1919, developed his ideas under the impact of Mussolini in the late-1920s; but soon even his ideas seemed too moderate to the younger generation. The most important fascist body was the Arrow Cross Party of Greenshirts, founded by Ferenc Szálasi in the 1930s. This achieved considerable popularity. Yet Horthy, who was made regent for life in 1937, remained in control, though he bowed to Nazi pressure and took Hungary into the Second World War at the end of 1940. Szálasi came to power only briefly, after

Horthy tried to make peace with the allies in 1944, but was tried and executed after the war.

b) Turkey

The Ottoman Empire, the 'sick man of Europe' before 1914, finally came to an end after the war. Its imperial possessions were distributed among the victors, but Kemal Ataturk, who had saved Istanbul from capture during the Gallipoli campaign, organised national resistance to the partition of Anatolia in Turkey itself. In so doing he became popular enough to lead a revolt against the Sultan and to become life president of a new Turkish republic. His regime was in fact a dictatorship, and there are definite similarities with the European dictatorships often characterised as fascist. Yet the label is seldom applied to Ataturk, perhaps because his primary drive was to westernise Turkey and destroy Islamic institutions, aims which had no parallel elsewhere. Indeed his campaign against Islam even led him, in sharp contrast to fascist regimes, to give women equal rights with men in education, employment and politics. His regime also looked for support, in the form of loans during the depression, from the Soviet Union.

c) Spain

After the First World War, Spanish society was dangerously divided. In fact, such division was nothing new, as there was a long history in Spain of exploitation, bitter protests and civil strife. Yet now unemployment and falling wages seemed to herald actual class warfare, especially when anarchist trade unions turned to strikes, terrorism and murder. In addition, nationalist feeling was aggrieved when, in July 1921, the Spanish army suffered a humiliating defeat by rebels in Morocco, with the loss of 17,000 lives. It came as little surprise, therefore, when in September 1923 the exiting regime collapsed: General Miguel Primo de Rivera set up a military dictatorship. He banned political parties and jailed or exiled his opponents. He was certainly aware of Mussolini's 'March on Rome' and admired the Italian dictator; but in fact his regime had little in common with the regimes usually described as fascist. He was not as repressive, expansionist or cruel as Hitler or Mussolini. He did not kill any of his opponents and did not ban trade unions, though insisting that they stay out of politics. Nor did he found any political party. Furthermore, he did not hang on to power at all costs: indeed he resigned at the start of 1930, leaving a highly unstable country.

Republican feeling was growing, and in 1931 the king, Alfonso XIII, fled to France. Elections then resulted in a moderate socialist coalition, which was also anti-clerical, separating church and state, limiting religious influence in schools and making divorce legal. Yet from the beginning the new republican regime was ringed by enemies. To the right were the church, the army and wealthy landowners and industrialists; to the left were the anarchists, who organised a series of political strikes and acts of terrorism. Fresh elections at the end of 1933 then resulted in a victory for the right. Employers took the opportunity to cut wages, and the left responded by setting up workers' committees in a so-called 'October Revolution' in 1934. Mindful of the overthrow of the left in Italy and Germany, the Spanish left opted for resolute defiance. However, troops from the Spanish Foreign Legion brutally crushed the insurrection within two weeks, with about 4,000 casualties. The result was that politics were polarised as never before, and in the 1936 general election, fought in a frenzied atmosphere, centre groups did not seem to exist: the left combined in a Popular Front, winning almost five million votes, while the right formed a coalition and polled four million. Spain's generals, to whom democracy meant little more than disorder, then decided to act. Appalled at the violence in the country and also concerned that the Popular Front victory might encourage separatist groups in Catalan and elsewhere to break away, they attempted to seize power. In fact, they did not have complete control over the army, and as a result their coup was only partially effective. A civil war broke out. General Franco was proclaimed head of state in September 1936, but it was not until April 1939 that he was recognised as master of all Spain.

The civil war saw substantial intervention from outside: Stalin aided the republican forces, while Mussolini and Hitler helped Franco. It is not surprising, therefore, that Franco is sometimes identified with the fascists. Certainly many of those who went to Spain to fight against him were convinced that they were fighting fascism. Whether the regime should be called fascist is examined in the next chapter, but it should be noted that Franco never called himself a fascist and drew his ideology largely from the church. Other groups on the Spanish right can more definitely be called fascist, in particular the Falange, which had been founded in 1934 by the former dictator's son, José Antonio Primo de Rivera. Mussolini, it should be noted, supported the Falange financially. Nevertheless this group was small, and its romantic rhetoric and corporatist ideas seemed to attract only university students: to the mass of the population its imitation of Italian Fascism was foreign and thus unpopular. In the 1936 elections, Falange candidates won only 44,000 votes, 0.7 per cent of the total. It is true that it did a good deal to create the disorder which led to the generals' intervention and that in the early period of the civil war many thousands joined its militia. But Franco, while pragmatically utilising Falange support, skilfully neutralised its influence in April 1937 by merging it with the Carlists, a monarchist party of the right.

d) Portugal

Portugal had the least developed economy in western Europe, as well as the highest illiteracy rate, and her politics were notoriously unstable. A democracy had been set up in 1910, when the last monarch fled the country, but over the next quarter century there were around 25 coups, and in 1926 rule by the army began. In 1928 the military president invited Antonio Salazar to become Minister of Finance; and few years later he was Prime Minister and virtual dictator, a position he occupied for the next 40 years.

In the early-1930s Salazar set up a one-party state, based on the National Union, complete with security police. He drafted an authoritarian and corporate constitution, which was accepted by plebiscite, his aim being to create a New State (*Estado Novo*). Nevertheless this is generally considered to have been a right-wing conservative regime, basing its actions squarely on Catholicism, though with a few fascist trappings, including a Corporative Chamber. There was no cult of personality around Salazar, who was a recluse, rarely appearing in public; and nor was there any militarisation of society. Corroboration for this interpretation came in 1932 when Rolao Preto set up a definite fascist party, the blue-shirted National Syndicalists. This group put forward extreme nationalist policies and combined left- and right-wing ideas, and its followers included those who wanted a more dynamic, modern and heroic country. But in 1934 Salazar acted, outlawing the movement and sending Preto into exile.

e) Greece

Greek politics lacked stability after the First World War. In particular there was no consensus on the basic form of government to be adopted. In 1924-35 there was a series of short-lived republican governments, but then George I became king for the second time. In 1936 the king allowed the right-wing General Metaxas to form a government, despite the fact that he had won only four per cent of the votes at the recent elections. Metaxas then utilised an outbreak of strikes, and fear of communism generally, to justify seizing political power: a new corporate state replaced the parliament and all political parties were dissolved. While it is true that he adopted some of the trappings of fascism, including the fascist salute, his regime is generally described as a right-wing military dictatorship. His primary efforts were devoted to improving military organisation. Metaxas himself said that his regime was closer to Salazar's in Portugal than to Mussolini's or Hitler's. Certainly the Italian felt no identity with him, Italian troops attempting - unsuccessfully - to overrun Greece in 1940. It was another politician, George Mercouris, who chose the fascist path, setting up the Greek National Socialist Party in the mid-1930s, without any success.

f) Poland

Poland, which had been partitioned three times in the eighteenth century, became an independent state again in 1918. The allies were determined that it should survive, and even provided access to the sea via a 'corridor' which divided East Prussia from the rest of Germany. Yet though the allies decided one border, with Germany, the remainder were determined by force of arms. The Poles fought six border wars in three years. These served to heighten nationalist feeling and to further militarise society. In addition, there were severe economic problems, including hyper-inflation. It may be thought, therefore, that Poland was likely to follow Italy into fascist dictatorship, especially since many were fearful of the Soviet Union and since there were no democratic traditions. The new constitution of 1921 worked badly and no coherent party system emerged: soon there were over 20 political parties among the Poles and over 30 among the minorities. The state was marked by corruption, inefficiency and violence.

In 1926 the war hero General Pilsudski led an army coup, forcing both the president and prime minister to resign. He set up what is sometimes called a semi-fascist dictatorship. Parliament and the political parties remained in being, but only as a facade. Real power lay with Pilsudski. On the other hand, repression did not affect the mass of the population. Pilsudski's real aim was not to follow any prescribed model of dictatorship but simply to keep Poland independent, despite the ambitions of her two overmighty neighbours, Germany and the Soviet Union. Also he founded no political party, and, like several dictators elsewhere but unlike Mussolini and Hitler, he looked to Catholicism to justify his regime rather than to any new ideology. It therefore seems best to describe his rule as a military and conservative - rather than fascist - dictatorship. After his death in 1935, Poland was controlled by a group of generals. Problems then began to multiply, especially as the German minority turned to Nazism.

4 Monarchical Dictatorships

a) Yugoslavia

A unified South Slav (Yugoslav) state, composed of Serbs, Croats and Slovenes, was set up at the end of 1918 under the Serb king, Alexander. But from the beginning it experienced bitter disputes between Serbs and Croats, which culminated in shooting incidents in the parliament. Then, in 1929, Alexander set up a royal dictatorship. He admired Mussolini, and perhaps drew inspiration from him, but his regime was unlike the Italian's in many ways. Critics believed that he was insufficiently a national leader, judging that he was too closely identified with the Serbs to dispense impartial justice; and in 1934 he was assassinated by an agent of Ustase, an extreme Croatian nationalist organisation which collaborated with the Germans and Italians during the Second World War. It was the Ustase movement which was the closer to fascism; the government itself must be considered a more traditional right-wing movement.

b) Romania

Romania gained as a result of the peace treaties, but nationalist feelings were kept at a high pitch because her neighbours wanted lost territories returned. In addition, communist propaganda caused disturbances and anti-Semitism was widespread. In this situation the new democratic constitution of 1923 never functioned effectively, and politics were notoriously corrupt. Fascist-like groups undoubtedly existed, the most important being the paramilitary Legion of the Archangel Michael, subsequently known as the Iron Guard, founded by the religious mystic Corneliu Codreanu in 1927. Its members wore characteristic green shirts and gave the Roman salute: sometimes they even used the word 'fascist' to describe themselves, though theirs was a more semi-religious movement than elsewhere. A decade later it was the third largest party in the country, but in 1938 a coup was staged by the power-hungry king, Carol II, an admirer of Mussolini. All political parties were then banned, and Codreanu was murdered in prison. In 1940 the Iron Guard staged an uprising and the king was ousted, but General Antonescu took power, as self-styled *Conducator,* and allied Romania with Germany. This was another essentially conservative dictatorship. Yet the Germans would not help the nearest thing the country had to a fascist group: Hitler advised Antonescu to crush the Iron Guard, and subsequently helped him to do so. The only time Romania was actually a fascist state - providing that fascism and Nazism are equated - was when it became a satellite of the Third Reich.

5 Germany

a) Nazi failure, 1918-28

Many Germans found it hard to accept the allied victory in November 1918. After all, defeat was announced when the German armies were a hundred miles into enemy territory and when there was not a single allied soldier in the fatherland. For many, including a young corporal, Adolf Hitler, the news of defeat was traumatic: 'everything went black before my eyes as I staggered back to my ward and buried my aching head between the blankets and pillow. ... The following days were terrible to bear and the nights still worse. ... During these nights my hatred increased, hatred for the originators of this dastardly crime'.[7] The 'November Criminals' were the Social Democrats who, forming a government just before the armistice, were widely believed to have pulled Germany out of a war which could still have been won. They had stabbed the country in the back. In these special circumstances, the new regime seemed to lack legitimacy: it was patriotic to be a rebel.

The new Weimar republic thus got off to the worst possible start. Its constitution was a model of democratic principles, but the spirit to operate it successfully did not exist. Germans had had little experience of democracy. Admittedly Bismarck had instituted universal male suffrage in 1871, but the electors chose only the Reichstag, a debating chamber: the members of the government were chosen by the Emperor, who alone could dismiss them. Many Germans in 1919 were not democrats, and certainly the overwhelming majority of those with power in society - including industrialists and landowners, civil servants and army officers - were not. Furthermore the republic was damned by association with the Treaty of Versailles, which created a whole host of nationalist grievances. Germany lost about 13 per cent of her land and population, together with all her overseas colonies; her army was limited to a mere 100,000 men; a large, unspecified sum in reparations had to be paid; Germany was blamed for causing the war; and there was to be a foreign army of occupation in the Rhineland for 15 years. The republican government had little choice but to sign the treaty. Yet they were blamed for doing so.

In addition, the government had to cope with severe postwar economic problems, and, when there was a delay with reparations payments, with a French occupation of the Ruhr which led to a disastrous hyper-inflation in 1923. At a stroke the savings (but also the debts) of the middle classes were wiped out. The very survival of the democratic regime was in grave jeopardy in 1919-23. At the beginning of this period, in 1919, there had been an attempted communist coup (the Spartakist rising), which had been defeated by irregular bands of ex-soldiers, the Free Corps; then, in 1920 there had been an attempt by Free Corps units in Berlin to seize power (the Kapp putsch), which a general strike of workers had defeated, after the government fled the capital in fear. The regime survived, but only very narrowly and only because its enemies, to left and right, cancelled each other out, not because of its own strength or popularity. Then, in 1923, there were further attempts at dictatorship. Hitler, leader of the National Socialist German Workers' Party, surrounded a meeting of politicians in a Munich beer hall with his Brownshirts and declared both the regional Bavarian government and the federal government in Berlin to be at an end: he would march on the capital and head a new regime.

There are clear similarities between the situations in Germany and Italy. In both there were communist threats, acute nationalist discontents, economic problems and democratic inexperience and unpopularity. Furthermore the war had exacerbated problems in both countries, producing a large number of ex-servicemen who proved ready recruits for irregular private armies, whether they were called *squadristi* or Free Corps. There is also a clear parallel in the blind eye turned by the official forces of law and order to violent anti-communism. When asked if he knew that there were gangs of murderers in Munich, the head of police in 1923 replied: 'Yes, but not enough of them'.[8] Also there are parallels between Hitler (1889-1945) and Mussolini. Both had fought in the war, though Hitler with considerably more distinction, winning the Iron Cross (first class); and both combined left- and right-wing ideas. The original programme of the Nazi party referred to 'breaking the shackles of finance capital'. Mussolini appealed to all the 'people of Italy', and Hitler promised to form a *Volksgemeinschaft,* a community that transcended class barriers. Admittedly Mussolini had been one of the founders of the Fascists in Italy, but when Hitler first joined the German Workers' Party in 1919 it had only 54 members. There were also personal similarities between the two men, in that both were rootless individuals, at first unsuccessful, to whom a radical political commitment gave meaning and direction. Both were also rousing orators and expert propagandists, and they were entirely ruthless.

There is little doubt that Hitler modelled himself to some degree on the Italian. Looking back on 1923, Hitler recalled: 'I confess frankly, I conceived the deepest admiration for the great man south of the Alps, who in passionate love for his people refused to make terms with the internal enemies of Italy, but sought their destruction by all ways and means. What will place Mussolini among the great of the earth is his determination not to share Italy with Marxism'.[9] Hitler's brown-shirted SA (*Sturmabtteilung*) was his version of the Italian Blackshirts, and like Mussolini he borrowed from earlier nationalist and *Völkisch* groups, adopting the swastika and the greetings of *'Heil'* and *'Sieg Heil'* ('Hail' and 'Hail victory'). Certainly the projected March on Berlin was an attempt to copy the March on Rome - or, rather, the glorious image of the event which Fascist propaganda portrayed. Yet whereas Mussolini was made Prime Minister, Hitler was sentenced to five years' imprisonment in Landsberg prison, the minimum sentence, it should be noted, to which the sympathetic judiciary could sentence him. Here Hitler decided to change his tactics: 'Instead of working to achieve power by an armed coup, we shall have to hold our noses and enter the Reichstag against the Catholic and Marxist deputies'.[10] Consciously he was departing from Mussolini's methods, but in reality he was following the Italian's combination of legality and violence.

Released from prison early, in late 1924, Hitler had a lean time of it at first, especially since in 1924-29 the Weimar Republic finally seemed to be enjoying success. The French left the Ruhr in 1925, and the Dawes plan (1924) and the Young Plan (1929) scaled down reparations. In 1926 Germany entered the League of Nations; and it was even arranged that the French would evacuate the Rhineland in 1930, ahead of schedule. In addition, inflation was overcome and these were years of economic prosperity. Output from the factories increased by 17 per cent in 1925-29. In the elections of 1928 the Nazis won only 2.5 per cent of the votes and a mere handful of seats. Perhaps, had prosperity been maintained, the republic might not only have survived but become popular. Yet, as it was, the economic depression from 1929 onwards provided ideal circumstances for the Nazis.

b) Nazi success, 1929-33

Even in the prosperous mid-1920s there were danger signs for the republic. In 1925 the German people had elected as President the war hero Paul von Hindenburg, more of a kaiser-substitute than a suitable figurehead for a democratic republic. Furthermore, no coherent party system emerged: proportional representation allowed dozens of parties to gain seats, and no single group could hope to gain an overall majority. Most important of all, economic prosperity was dangerously dependent on foreign loans, particularly from the Americans; and, as a result, the stock market crash on Wall Street in October 1929 had disastrous consequences. Henceforth no new loans could be negotiated and short-term loans were recalled. Soon Germany was in the throes of the Great Depression. By 1932 exports had fallen by over 50 per cent and industrial production by over 40 per cent, compared with 1928, and unemployment mounted month after month, reaching almost 6 million by 1932. By this time one in every three workers was unemployed and at least half of German families had a member out of work. To make matters worse, there were millions more on short time. No one was immune, blue-collar or white-collar worker, man or woman.

Traditional governments had no answer to these economic problems. All they could recommend was that expenditure be scaled back in line with falling tax revenue; but this issue led to a fatal split in March 1930 between liberals and Social Democrats, the latter refusing to support cuts in unemployment benefit. The resignation of Chancellor Müller and the appointment, in his place, of Heinrich Brüning was the beginning of the end for German democracy. Henceforth neither Brüning nor any successor could find a majority for his measures in the Reichstag: instead, government was carried on by Presidential decree, authorised by article 48 of the constitution. In the period 1930-32 109 emergency decrees were passed but only 29 ordinary laws, and in the same period the Reichstag met more and more infrequently: 93 times in 1930 and 41 times the following year, while in 1932 it was called together on only 13 occasions. Democracy was grinding to a halt.

It had originally been envisaged that emergency decrees, consequent upon parliamentary deadlock, would be a stop-gap, pending new elections which would restore a majority. But fresh elections only made matters worse - or better, from the Nazi perspective. Even in 1928 the Nazis polled well in the depressed rural areas, where wages were lagging far behind those in industry, and now there were far more discontented people to whom Hitler and his party could appeal. In September 1930 the well organised Nazi party won 18 per cent of the total vote, becoming the second largest party in the Reichstag, and in July 1932 - amid escalating violence on the streets, for which they were responsible - they received a massive 37 per cent (13.75 million votes and 230 seats). No party had ever received more votes. (For details of who voted for the Nazis, see pages 97-98.) Hitler was undoubtedly benefiting from a polarisation in German politics which had been underway for several years. Indeed in July 1932, 52 per cent of electors voted either for the Communist Party (KPD) on the left or the Nazi party on the right. Admittedly the KPD and the Social Democratic Party (SPD) together polled more than the Nazis, but there was no co-operation between them: indeed the Communists - very foolishly, as we can see now - looked upon the Social Democrats as their main enemy.

It is often said that proportional representation aided the Nazi cause, and certainly it had allowed them to gain an initial foothold in the Reichstag, but in July 1932 it harmed their performance. Under a first-past-the-post system they might well have achieved an overall majority: as it was, Hitler, though leader of the largest single party, was not invited to form a government. Indeed perhaps his chance had gone, for in November 1932 fresh elections, which drained the party's coffers, saw the Nazi vote fall back to 33 per cent, with 196 seats.

In fact, Hitler had not long to wait. The Chancellor, Franz von Papen, believing he could control Hitler now that his support was waning, offered him a government post; but the Nazi leader boldly refused to accept any other office than that of Chancellor. Indeed he insisted that he should have the same sort of position Mussolini had occupied after the March on Rome. Papen was then replaced by General Schleicher, who ambitiously - but vainly - aimed to split the Nazis by appealing to the more socialistically-minded among them. Yet Papen was determined to oust his rival Schleicher and, in pursuit of this aim, played a last desperate card: he offered Hitler a deal whereby the two of them would head a coalition government, but this time he accepted that Hitler would be Chancellor, with Papen himself as Vice-Chancellor. Reluctantly the ageing President Hindenburg agreed: only thus, it seemed, could Germany be made safe from communism. Hitler, the sworn enemy of the Weimar Republic, became its Chancellor on 30 January 1933, as a result of political intrigue.

Hitler was still not a dictator, and there seemed little reason to suppose that he would last longer than any previous chancellor. There were only two Nazis, besides himself, in the twelve-man cabinet, and the Nazis did not have a majority in the Reichstag. Thus his position was very similar to Mussolini's, on being made Prime Minister in 1922; but it took Hitler even less time than the Italian to supplant democracy entirely. The Reichstag fire of 27 February 1933 created the ideal 'red scare', and Hitler utilised it to suspend civil liberties and to use the powers of the state, as well as of the Nazi party, to intimidate opponents in elections the following month. There were 69 political murders during the campaign. Even so, the Nazis still did not win an overall majority (gaining 44 per cent of the vote and 288 seats) - and a majority of two-thirds was needed to change the constitution and give Hitler dictatorial powers. Yet the Enabling Bill was duly passed by 444 votes to 94. Hitler made tactical promises to win the votes of the Catholic Centre Party and, moreover, he had surrounded the makeshift chamber with his militia, creating an atmosphere of extreme menace, as Mussolini had done over the Acerbo law (see page 45). The Weimar Republic was finally at an end.

c) Assessment

Events in Germany in the 1930s were similar to those in Italy a decade earlier. In each case there were the same general circumstances: economic dislocation, a communist threat, nationalist grievances and extreme democratic weakness. Indeed we may well say that in both countries democracy collapsed, rather than being overthrown. Very few Germans thought that democracy could be brought back to life. Some wished to bring back the monarchy, in the form of the ex-Kaiser's son, while others thought in terms of drastically reducing the franchise and setting up a presidential dictatorship. People wanted immediate, drastic solutions, not a continuance of democratic impotence. The Hungarian writer Arthur Koestler described Germany at this time as 'a disintegrating society thirsting for faith'. Another parallel is that the professional politicians thought that they could control the man who soon became their master.

It might seem, therefore, that there was a definite 'fascist road to power', especially since both Hitler and Mussolini pursued similar tactics, for instance by holding out for the top political post, instead of accepting a subordinate office, and also by skilfully posing as moderate. Mussolini dissociated himself from the *Ras*, Hitler from the more radical and socialist wing of the Nazi party, led by Gregor Strasser. Only in this way could they hope to win important financial support from capitalists and reassure men like Giolitti in Italy and Papen in Germany that they could be tamed by power. However, while posing as moderates, they had no scruples about using violence on a grand scale. They also used propaganda with great sophistication to hammer home simple messages, exaggerating the communist threat and playing upon nationalist hopes and fears. Hitler, for instance, made much of Germany's 'bleeding border' in the east. Above all, they spoke with a refreshing and infectious confidence and offered the prospect of national resurgence. While traditional politicians tried to explain and excuse their failures, Hitler and Mussolini projected an image of bold determination. As a result, many believed that they should at least be given a try. After all, could things get any worse?

The Fascist and Nazi routes to power are undoubtedly similar. This is due to several factors. There were comparable situations in the two countries; in addition, Mussolini was prepared to give advice and money, and Hitler to take it; and, furthermore, the two leaders had much in common. Nevertheless there was no uniformity between the two movements, and the similarity is partly explained by coincidence, as with the misguided tactics of those who sought to control the party leaders. There are also key differences between Hitler and Mussolini. The Italian was ideologically an opportunist, but Hitler took ideas far more seriously. No doubt his beliefs were irrational and simplistic, but he did have fixed ideas, about, for instance, the importance of race. Not only did he believe in German - or more generally in 'Aryan' - racial superiority, but he believed in the existence of sub-races, the lowest of whom were the Jews. Hitler has been called 'the greatest anti-Semite in the history of the world',[11] and he gained considerable popularity by proclaiming that the Jews were the authors of all Germany's ills, a view vaguely believed by many. Hitler was also far more systematic than Mussolini in his aims for foreign policy (see page 83).

Hitler undoubtedly admired Mussolini. On the other hand, this emotion was not reciprocated. Above all, Mussolini could not take Hitler's anti-Semitism seriously. The Italian insisted that there was only a superficial resemblance between Fascism and Nazism - an important warning that we should not exaggerate the coherence of generic fascism.

6 Austria

One factor that divided Hitler and Mussolini in the mid-1930s was the future of Austria. Should it remain under the influence of Italy, as Mussolini desired, or should it unite with Germany? In this arena, Fascism and Nazism - whatever similarities may be discerned between them - were enemies, not allies.

The survival of Austria as an independent state had seemed unlikely ever since the harsh Treaty of St Germain (1919), by which Austria lost not only her Empire but about a third of her German-speaking population. Hence the new republic was a small, land-locked state with a population of less than 8 million, over 2 million of whom lived in Vienna. No real sense of 'Austrian' nationality existed, and a constituent assembly even voted to join Germany, though the peace treaties forbade such a union (*Anschluss*). It seemed that the Austrians were only united in their determination not to be Austrian.

Austrian weakness was patently obvious. There was disastrous hyper-inflation in 1922, and also endemic violence. There were also frequent clashes between private armies, the right-wing *Heimwehr* (originally rural defence leagues against looting ex-soldiers) and the left-wing *Schutzbund*, resulting in serious riots in the capital in July 1927 when 88 were killed. It was at this point that the ruling Christian Social Party virtually adopted the *Heimwehr* as its paramilitary wing. Then came the economic depression of the early-1930s, intensified in Austria by the collapse of a leading bank, the Credit Anstalt, in May 1931. Depression, as elsewhere, boosted the fortunes of the left, already strong in 'Red Vienna'. In November 1930 the Social Democrats won 42 per cent of the vote and became the largest party in the Reichstag with 72 seats. The Christian Social party won 62 seats, but were kept in power by the support of deputies on the far right. In this defensive position, the government acquiesced in, or even supported, the attempts of the *Heimwehr* to intimidate the socialists. The days of democracy seemed numbered.

After a series of short-lived governments, Engelbert Dollfuss became leader of the Christian Socials and Chancellor of Austria in 1932. Yet he and his right-wing allies had a majority of only one, and rather than call new elections he engineered a coup in March 1933. Soon he banned the *Schutzbund* and the communist party, on the left, and the Austrian Nazi Party, on the right. In addition, Austrians were forbidden to demonstrate or go on strike, and freedom of speech and of the press was ended. This was the first stage in his revolution. The second came after a left-wing reaction. Members of the *Schutzbund*, whose leaders had been arrested, staged a general strike in February 1934. The result was fierce fighting in several cities. In Vienna, for instance, the *Heimwehr* bombarded two blocks of workers' flats, Karl Marx House and Goethe House, which the socialist city council had built. Perhaps as many as 1,500 men, women and children were killed. In this situation Dollfuss imposed a stricter dictatorship, banning the socialist party and the trade unions and issuing a new constitution, by which political parties were replaced by professional corporations, though special privileges were given to the Catholic church.

It is not easy to find a label to adequately describe the new regime. Certainly Mussolini had been supporting the *Heimwehr* financially since 1927 and regarded himself as the patron of the new Austria, and indeed many historians have emphasised the specifically Italian contribution to the overthrow of Austrian democracy. There also seems to have been a European dimension. All the vital ingredients making for generic fascism seemed present in Austria: nationalist grievances, economic dislocation, the threat from the left and a weak democratic regime, combined moreover with prewar, proto-fascist traditions of racialism and authoritarianism. However, others emphasise the degree to which developments reflected specifically Austrian traditions. Dollfuss himself gave a lot of prominence to Catholicism, which he hoped would distinguish his regime from the Italian. In addition, it is said that the corporatist nature of the constitution was home-grown, stemming from the works of Austrian thinkers like Othmar Spann, not foisted on Austria by Mussolini. Probably there are elements of truth in both interpretations: the term 'Austrofacsism' has been coined to represent a form of fascism similar to but different from others, an alliance between clerical conservatism, stemming mainly from local soil, and the largely imported fascist principles of the *Heimwehr*.

It is clear, however, that the regime was not Nazi in inspiration. This became even more clear on 25 July 1934, when the Austrian nazis attempted a coup. The army crushed the revolt, but Dollfuss himself was captured and shot, and virtual civil war followed between the Austrian fascists and the Austrian nazis. Kurt von Schuschnigg became the new Chancellor, but his authority waned as German influence grew - in both Austria and Italy. Mussolini became reconciled to the inevitable, and in March 1938 German troops invaded Vienna. The *Anschluss* took place, Austria becoming merely a province of Greater Germany.

7 Conclusion

How important was fascism in the eclipse of democracy in Europe between the wars? This is a very difficult question to answer. It is necessary to keep several balls in the air at the same time: we have to consider not only all the reasons why democracy failed in a dozen countries but also to ask 'what is fascism - a generic movement or a series of essentially separate political groups?' Without defining fascism, we cannot say which movements were fascist or investigate their role in overthrowing democracy, but the fact is that there is no generally accepted definition of fascism. Therefore we have to consider all the parties which in this period were undemocratic and fascist-like (a vague term, deliberately chosen) - or as many of them as are practicable in a chapter this size. (Some possibly fascist groups, for instance in Norway, Finland, Latvia and Estonia, have been omitted, leaving scope for further reading.)

Of the movements that have been covered, many have been classified as right-wing conservative rather than fascist. It does seem that not all authoritarian regimes should be called fascist. There are at least two reasons for this: first, many were buttressed not by any new ideology but by traditional Catholicism; and, second, they had to cope with opposition from more genuinely fascist groups. Certainly it seems that only two fascist-like parties - the Fascists in Italy and the Nazis in Germany - remained in power for any length of time. Nevertheless, given the lack of hard-and-fast definitions, there is scope here for disagreement. After all, even regimes which do not appear to be genuinely fascist often borrowed fascist trappings, for instance by the use of mass rallies and elaborate ceremonials. Those who take a 'soft' definition of fascism, therefore, identifying it with almost all non-communist authoritarian groups, will tend to maximise the number of fascist movements, while those who adopt a 'harder' definition, specifying a larger number of criteria to be satisfied, will do the opposite.

What were the main causes of democracy's failure? If we pick out the four issues of communist threat, nationalist grievances, economic dislocation and democratic inefficiency, then this common framework may well tend to emphasise the importance of generic fascism as a factor in the overthrow of democracy. After all, many fascist-like groups tended to gain support because of these four factors. If, on the other hand, we pick out separate, national causes, then the importance of any general explanation will be diminished. This will also be the case if we emphasise 'contingent factors'. But the fact is that there are always local causes of political change, peculiar to particular areas and reflecting their histories. Nor should we ignore the importance of luck, or the actions of powerful individuals, in explaining any historical event: if we do, then historical developments will appear, quite unrealistically, to have been inevitable. Similarly, there were bound to be some common causes, especially since the whole continent had been affected by the First World War. In addition, groups in one country were aware of what was happening elsewhere and reacted accordingly. Yet neither general European factors, on their own, nor solely national or contingent factors will explain what happened. Hence our explanation of democracy's failure cannot be completely clear-cut: we have to weigh up the different factors, and in no two countries is the 'balance' likely to be the same.

It may seem that Mussolini's influence, in encouraging and even financing regimes outside Italy, favours the importance of generic fascism. Yet Mussolini's support was sometimes counterproductive, making local fascist parties seem foreign, inauthentic and thus unpopular. This was certainly the case with the British Union of Fascists. Fascist-like parties tended to be most popular where they were - or at least seemed to be - native responses to national problems. This was the case in Italy, and also in Germany. Mussolini gave considerable aid to the Nazis, and Hitler seemed almost to hero-worship him for a time; but few could doubt that the Nazis built upon German historical traditions or that they were acutely aware of local grievances.

How similar were the Fascists and Nazis in their rise to power? Perhaps the best summary is to say that there was a family resemblance between Mussolini and Hitler as they strove for power. Both used a combination of legality and violence; both were skilful and unscrupulous in exploiting unexpected circumstances; and both knew what they wanted and were not to be fobbed off with less than real power. But perhaps they were more like cousins than brothers, and certainly they were not twins.

Hence there were important similarities and differences between the different fascist-like groups. Was there a 'fascist road to power'? Perhaps our answer should be that of the Dutchman van der Lubbe. When on trial for starting the Reichstag fire, he replied to most questions with the phrase 'yes - no'. Yes (in certain respects there were significant similarities between the different 'fascist' groups, in their response to the problems they faced and in the ways they attempted to come to power) and No (in other respects they were all unique, particularly because of historical and contingent factors). This is not a comforting conclusion for those who like simple answers. But historical truth - like any other form of truth - is, as Oscar Wilde once said, rarely pure and never simple.

References

1 E.H. Carr, *Twenty Years' Crisis* (Macmillan, 1946), p. 230.
2 R.J.B. Bosworth, 'The British Press, the Conservatives, and Mussolini, 1920-34', *Journal of Contemporary History*, vol. 5, no. 2, 1970, p. 167.
3 F.L. Carsten, *The Rise of Fascism* (Batsford, 1967), p. 48.
4 Philip Morgan, *Italian Fascism 1919-1945* (Macmillan, 1995), p. 12.
5 Ibid, p. 52.
6 Denis Mack Smith, *Mussolini* (Granada, 1981), p. 86.
7 Alan Bullock, *Hitler: A Study in Tyranny* (Penguin, 1962), p. 60.
8 Ibid, p. 63.
9 Elizabeth Wiskemann, *The Rome-Berlin Axis* (Fontana, 1966), p. 22.
10 Niall Rothnie, *National Socialism in Germany* (Macmillan, 1987), p. 22.
11 W. Rubenstein, *A History of the Jews in the English-Speaking World: Great Britain* (Macmillan, 1995), p. 279.

Answering Essay Questions on 'The Rise of Fascism'

Essay questions on the rise of the fascists are common. Sometimes they focus on single regimes; but they can also adopt a wider approach. Consider the following examples:

1 Why did democracy collapse in so many European countries between 1918 and 1939?
2 Account for the rise of fascism between the two world wars.
3 Explain the rise to power of Mussolini and Hitler.
4 'Without communism, no fascism.' How far would you accept this dictum?

Every decent essay must have a beginning, a middle and an end. In the study guides in this book, advice will be given on each stage. First, the opening paragraph. Here you should aim to do several things: i) explain the meaning of the question, defining key terms and establishing the parameters of the question; ii) break the question down into several smaller and thus more manageable areas, on each of which you would subsequently write a paragraph; iii) briefly outline your argument or,

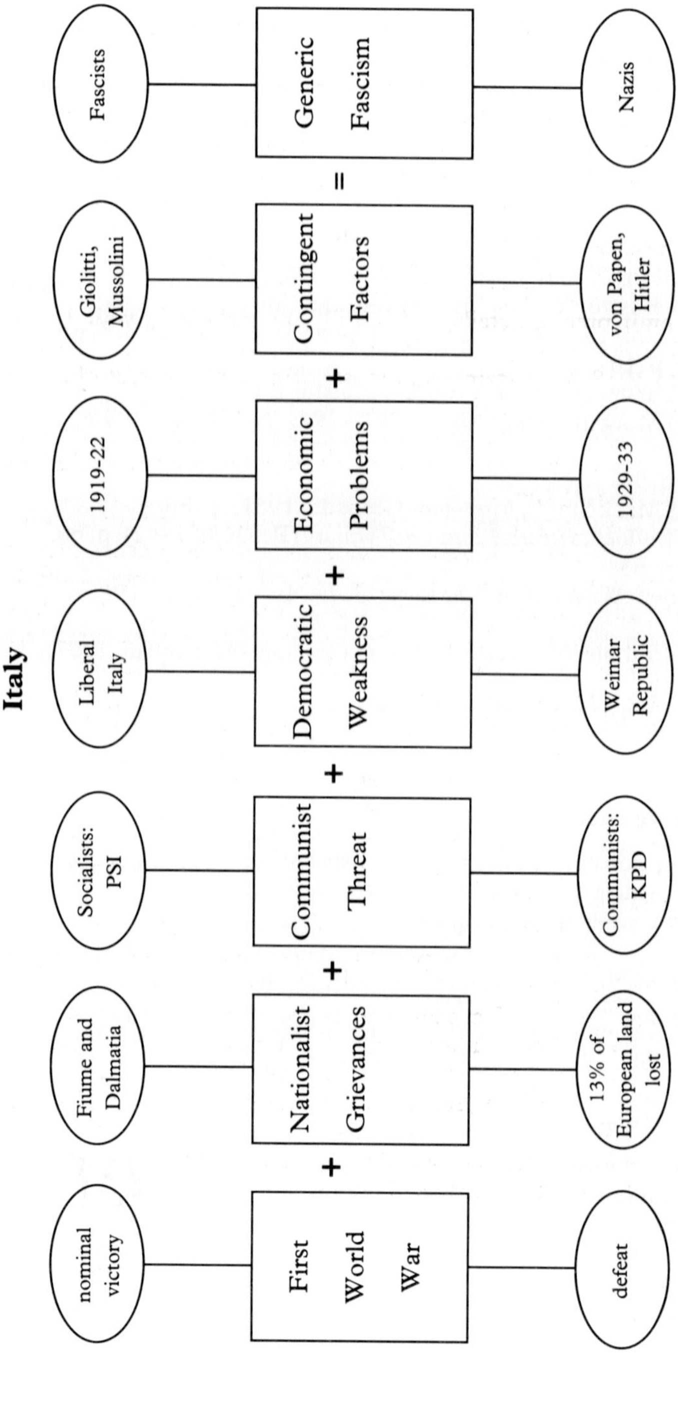

Summary - The Rise of Fascism

perhaps, several possible arguments. An opening paragraph on these lines should help you to avoid the two commonest errors in essay-writing, being irrelevant and giving narrative rather than analysis.

Consider question 1. The first thing to notice is that this is not specifically about fascism at all, though fascism is obviously important. Before writing the first paragraph, you might draw up two lists: first, of the countries where democracy collapsed, and, second, of the major factors which led to the collapse. Remember that, to get a good mark, you must not confine your answer to material from only Italy and Germany. On the other hand, you must not adopt such a broad brush that you omit precise details. What will you include in your list of factors? Remember that, in your search for explanations, you are not confined to 1918-39: certainly you must include the First World War and the Bolshevik Revolution. What will your overall argument be? Perhaps you may want to stress a combination of several factors as providing a reasonable explanation. How much prominence will you give to contingent factors?

Question 2 is also well worth tackling. Note that the 'rise of fascism' between the wars stemmed in part from pre-war developments. Hence you will need to have at least a paragraph drawn from chapter 2 of this book. You will also have to grapple with the meaning - or rather meanings - of 'fascism'. Try to strike a sensible balance between the contingent, historical, European-wide and country-specific factors.

Question 3 is a very popular and important issue. You might start by defining exactly when they achieved power: this will enable you to make the question much more concrete and specific. Always try to pinpoint exactly what you have to explain, before trying to do the explaining! Your overall argument could revolve round the issue of just how similar/dissimilar their paths to power were (whether they operated in similar political or economic circumstances, whether they used the same tactics and weapons, etc).

Question 4 has the virtue of being much more limited than the others in terms of subject-matter. One possible way of starting might be to put the quotation into your own (fuller and clearer) words, and to specify which countries you will focus on. You can of course bring in countries like Great Britain, where neither fascism nor communism was much of a threat. Perhaps the key point to make is that history is not a science: we can't conduct control experiments, eliminating one ingredient to observe the effects of its removal. All we can do is illustrate the importance of communism for fascist success and compare the importance of this factor with that of others.

CHAPTER 4

Fascism in Action

In this chapter we are concerned with fascist-like regimes. These must include Italy and Germany, where the Fascists and Nazis were in power for comparatively long periods, though whether other regimes qualify is more problematic. The aim is to assess what these regimes achieved and whether the similarities between them outweigh any differences. If they do, then a common label - 'fascist' - may well be applied to them, and we may gain a clearer understanding of this term. If they do not, then the concept of generic fascism must be questioned. (For the sake of clarity of analysis, certain overall issues - including the relationship of fascism to capitalism, modernisation and totalitarianism - are reserved for the next chapter.)

1 Italy and Germany: Political Affairs

a) Italy

By 1928 Mussolini was a dictator. He called himself a Fascist dictator, but his was a personal rather than a Fascist dictatorship, if by the latter is meant rule by the Fascist party. Indeed Mussolini was determined to control the party. Already, in 1923, he had created a Fascist Grand Council, which he dominated: only he could determine when it met, who sat on it and what was discussed. Now he ended elections within the party, so that all appointments were dependent on him. Potential rivals were neutralised. This was certainly the fate of two of the most powerful *Ras*: Roberto Farinacci from Cremona was first made secretary-general of the party and then dismissed, while Italo Balbo from Ferrara was exiled as governor of Libya. Leading figures in the party were henceforth chosen not for any personal distinction but for their total obedience to *Il Duce*. At the end of the 1920s many ex-*squadristi* were expelled from the party, and their places were taken by those who earlier would have been considered too conservative-minded to be Fascists. In short, Mussolini encouraged mass membership of the party. Being a Fascist was henceforth a passport to advancement rather than a sign of having any particular political ideas. By 1943 there were almost five million party members.

It was not an all-powerful dictatorship. After all, the monarchy still existed, the king retaining the theoretical right to dismiss Mussolini as head of government, and the church also had some power and influence. Nor did Mussolini have total control over the military. In addition, parliament was kept in being, even though it had no independence.

Within this system, Mussolini took actions to widen his powers. Nothing was done about the monarchy, but then it seemed that nothing need be done: Victor Emmanuel did not question *Il Duce*'s powers and was seldom even consulted. Probably Mussolini was waiting for him to die, and then he himself would become head of state, as well as head of government. However, the already weak powers of the parliament were diminished. In 1929 Mussolini changed the voting system: the electors were presented with a list of 400 carefully-selected names which they could accept or reject en bloc. Needless to say they accepted, and by huge majorities. Yet this made no essential difference, for it was Mussolini alone who made laws, the deputies merely shouting their assent. In 1939 he went a step further and abolished the parliament altogether. More significant was Mussolini's agreement with the Papacy in February 1929, the Lateran treaties. Pope Pius XI now recognised the Italian state. Mussolini thereby gained greater international prestige, and he hoped that henceforth Italian Catholics would be more reconciled to his rule. It seemed a great feat, and certainly the previous liberal governments had not been able to do a similar deal with the papacy. Yet there was little real substance to it. Mussolini paid a high price for the agreement: not only did he have to find £30 million, as compensation for the pope's lost lands, but the church had to be accorded a special position in Italy: religious education by priests was introduced into secondary schools; church marriage was officially recognised; and the salaries of the clergy had to be paid by the state. Furthermore, relations between church and state were never really good. Mussolini refused to kneel and kiss the Pope's hand on his first official visit to the Vatican city state; and there was then dissension about the suppression of 'Catholic Action', a youth organisation, which the Duce believed should be replaced by Fascist bodies. The church was critical of several aspects of Fascism and was particularly hostile towards the creed which Fascist youth had to repeat ('I believe in the genius of Mussolini, in our Holy Father Fascism, in the communion of its martyrs, in the conversion of Italians, and in the resurrection of the Empire'). The church opposed Mussolini's 1938 anti-Semitic measures (see page 81); and the following year the Pope made it clear that he regretted having signed the treaties.

Nevertheless there can be no doubt that it was a personal dictatorship. There was not even a proper cabinet. Ministers were simply given orders by Mussolini. (At least this was the theory, though sometimes he did not bother to give them any.) By 1933 Mussolini was not only Head of Government but the holder of 14 cabinet posts; and he was also head of all three armed services. As a final feature to his dictatorship, a 'cult of personality' was begun. Soon his picture was everywhere. In a new legal code, in 1931, it became a crime even to injure the prestige of the Duce. He was spoken of as 'our divine Duce' and his regime as an 'incarnation of God'. One of his admirers, Ottavio Dinale, said that, though his name was Benito Mussolini, he was really 'Alexander the Great and Caesar, Socrates and Pluto, Virgil and Lucretius, Horace and Tacitus, Kant and Nietzsche, Marx and Sorel,

Machiavelli and Napoleon, Garibaldi and the Unknown Soldier'.[1] Peasants were reported to kneel when he graced them with his presence and women held up their small children for him to bless. He was said to work 20 hours a day, though in fact he generally went to bed early.

The inevitable price to be paid for such a system was great inefficiency. Since everything was centralised on Mussolini, and he himself was not the superman that he pretended to be, there was bound to be muddle and waste. In particular there was no integrated administrative system in Italy, and often the state and party apparatuses overlapped. There was, for instance, the state army and the Fascist militia, which were kept separate. Mussolini boasted about this, calling it a system of twin beds, but it was a clumsy arrangement. There was also a high degree of incompetence and corruption, caused partly by the fact that Mussolini liked to surround himself with yes-men, who flattered him. He also had a particular liking for men shorter than himself.

Italy under Mussolini was a police state (that is, a state in which there is a police force not to protect citizens, but to protect the government and coerce the citizens). The OVRA, the Fascist secret police, was an integral part of the dictatorship. It has been estimated that, in a typical week, the OVRA conducted around 20,000 'visits', searches or arrests. During the entire regime 5,000 people were sentenced for political reasons to a total of 28,000 years imprisonment or banishment. In the period up to 1940, there were nine executions of political prisoners, with another 17 more during the war. Yet this record was not nearly as brutal as that of Nazi Germany. Payne judges that the Italian regime was 'brutal and repressive, but not murderous and bloodthirsty'.[2]

b) Germany

After the Enabling Act had given him emergency powers in March 1933, Hitler was concerned with *Gleichschaltung* (establishing effective centralised control). Unlike Mussolini, in the previous decade, he had no intention of pulling one tooth at a time, though he knew that he could not do all he wanted at once.

In May 1933 trade union premises were occupied and many of their leaders arrested. All unions were taken over by the DAF (the German Labour Front). In June and July 1933 the remaining political parties dissolved themselves. The Nazi Party was thus the only party with official existence in the state: anyone engaging in political activity outside its ranks was liable to three years in prison. Early the following year provincial governments and parliaments were abolished. The Ministry of the Interior - that is, the central government - controlled local affairs.

Yet Hitler had to take some care not to antagonise too many powerful people at the same time, including President Hindenburg, the churches, the army and industrialists. Hence he argued that revolution could not be a permanent condition. He did not want a revolution 'from below' - not now he was at the top. But to some - and especially Ernst Röhm, the leader of the SA - he was not being radical enough; and so Hitler moved against the SA in the Night of the Long Knives, on 30 June 1934: hundreds were killed, including Röhm. Like Mussolini, but more quickly and brutally, Hitler had moved against the radicals and rivals in his party. Like Mussolini too, Hitler was determined to enhance his personal power. Events conspired to help him. In August 1934, Hindenburg died and Hitler was able to combine the positions of Chancellor and President: he was the Führer, to whom the army had to take an oath of allegiance. Admittedly there was still friction with the Protestant and Catholic churches, and Hitler's 1933 Concordat with the Pope was even more of a sham than Mussolini's in 1929, but the German had undoubtedly achieved a position of constitutional supremacy which the Italian could not parallel. It was said that Germany's constitution was the will of the Führer. Nevertheless, a cult of personality, similar to that in Italy, was built around Hitler, transforming him into a superhuman, infallible figure. At the Nuremberg rally in 1934, Hans Frank declared that 'You are Germany! When you act, the Nation acts; when you judge, the people judge. Our gratitude is expressed in the promise to stand by you in good times and bad - come what may.' Soon it was said that Hitler embodied

> the highest synthesis of his race ... the universalism of Goethe, the depth of Kant, the dynamism of Hegel, the patriotism of Fichte, the genius of Frederick II, the realism of Bismarck, as well as the tumultuous inspiration of Wagner and the perspicacity of Spengler.[3]

The result, as in Italy, was a personal dictatorship. Hitler ceased to call cabinets from 1938, insisting that his will - and his alone - should prevail. It was not a Nazi party dictatorship. The party did not take over the state: instead, the two tended to exist in parallel. For instance, there was the old judicial system and a special Nazi court system, a dualism to be seen throughout Nazi Germany. There existed side by side the party apparatus and the state apparatus. Sometimes they were unified by particular individuals who held key positions in both. The same man, for instance, headed the party's agrarian organisation and was also Minister for Agriculture. But this tended to be luck rather than design. More often party and state overlapped, causing administrative confusion and personal rivalries, especially since the structure of the party was far from clear-cut, with party organs having overlapping functions. William Carr has described the structure of government in Nazi Germany as 'a complex mosaic of party and state agencies with ill-defined and overlapping jurisdictions, sometimes complementing each other, more often mutually antagonistic, all striving to obtain a monopoly of power in their own domain.'[4]

Perhaps Hitler encouraged such rivalry and competition, which left him as the sole arbiter; or perhaps he simply was not capable of administrative efficiency. Either way, it was his will that was supreme - when he chose to make it so. But, as in Italy, the price to be paid for this personal dictatorship was a good deal of muddle and inefficiency.

There are also similarities between Italy and Germany in that the latter also needed a secret political police, though the German equivalent of the OVRA was far more tyrannical. Formed in 1925 as an elite bodyguard for Hitler, the SS (*Schutz Staffeln*) grew in importance under Heinrich Himmler and in 1934 carried out the purge of the SA. The main function of its members, who had a reputation for total commitment and ruthlessness, was to deal with Germany's internal enemies, including communists and Jews. The SD, a special security service, was created within it to act as intelligence agents; and scarcely less feared in Germany was the Gestapo, the secret state police, also under Himmler's control.

2 Italy and Germany: Social and Economic Affairs

a) Italy

Mussolini insisted that his task was no less than the transformation of his country. There would be rapid economic and social progress, while in foreign affairs there would be a return to the glories of the Roman Empire. To achieve these ends, he would change the character of the Italian people: they would become more hard-working and serious, and less frivolous and critical. They would sleep less and be more concerned with duty than pleasure. In short, they would become more like their beloved Duce. What success did he have in these aims? How constructive and successful was his Fascism?

Of course no one understands economics, not even economists and certainly not amateurs like Mussolini or Hitler. Nevertheless, at first all went well economically: Italy was benefiting from the improvement in economic conditions which affected the whole of Europe in the mid-1920s. Mussolini introduced no fundamental economic changes. Indeed he was at pains to reassure capitalists that they would be safe under Fascism. In 1923, by dropping Giolitti's proposed campaign to end tax evasion, he convinced the employers' organisation, the *Confindustria*, that they should support him. They were further pleased when he banned trade unions in 1925 and outlawed strikes the following year. He also appointed an orthodox professor of economics, de Stefani, as treasury minister and privatised the telephone industry. Taxes were lowered, and government spending fell as a proportion of gross national product (GNP).

The most important change came - or seemed to come - in 1926, when a new Ministry of Corporations was formed. A corporation (composed of employers and employees) was to run each industrial sector under the benevolent eye of the state. This would be a constructive 'third way' between capitalism and communism. Yet no real corporations came into existence during Mussolini's rule, and the primary function of the new ministry seems to have been to endorse wage reductions. Real wages probably fell by around 10 per cent from 1925 to 1938. Hence the main effect of all this superstructure was simply to control Italian workers. In 1943 Mussolini lamented that the greatest tragedy of his life had been his inability to control 'false corporatists' who were really 'agents of capitalism'.[5]

In the absence of effective machinery, Mussolini fell back on the notion that economic problems could be overcome by an act of will. 'To live for me means struggle, risk, tenacity ... not submitting to fate, not even to ... our so-called deficiency in raw materials'.[6] Hence from 1925, seeking to make Italy self-sufficient in wheat, Mussolini began the 'battle for grain'. Large government grants were given to farmers to help them mechanise, and high prices were guaranteed. The annual harvest rose from about 5.5 million tonnes to over 7 million within a decade. This seems like a great success, but wine and olive oil production, for export, was harmed, and consumers had to pay more for bread than ever before. There was also a 'battle for the lira'. In 1926 Mussolini revalued the lira (from 140 to 90 to the pound sterling). His motivation was partly prestige: a strong lira was a status symbol. Yet it raised the price of Italian goods abroad, and so efforts were made at home to lower wages, in order to cut costs. Yet the prices of Italian goods abroad remained high: even Fiat exported fewer cars. Imported foodstuffs should have been cheaper, but Mussolini slapped high tariffs on foreign food. Indeed he initiated protection of the home market in general, in order to prevent cheap goods flooding in, and he encouraged the local production of import substitutes. Only heavy industry (steel, ship-building and armaments) gained, through the importation of tariff-free steel. Hence Mussolini did have a significant impact on the economy, but many believed that his economic 'victories' were scarcely worth the price that had to be paid. Similarly with land reclamation. The showpiece in this battle was the draining of the Pontine Marshes, whose malarial swamps were drained and transformed into small farms. Yet the amount of land reclaimed was small in comparison with the costs involved.

A third enterprise was the 'battle for births', launched in 1927. Mussolini wanted to increase the birth-rate. He felt very strongly about this, believing that an expanding population not only befitted a virile nation but would necessitate increased colonies, another sign of national strength. Mussolini insisted that bachelors should be heavily taxed, while tax relief should be available for those with children: indeed a married man with six children was to be exempt from all taxation.

Mussolini thought that 12 children per family was the ideal, and in 1933 he personally congratulated 93 mothers who between them had borne 1,300 children. Yet despite such efforts - and an attempted ban on women wearing trousers - the birth rate fell (from 26.7 per 1,000 of the population in 1930 to 23.5 10 years later). He also wanted Italians to return to the healthy countryside; but another half million moved to the cities.

An economic crisis for the regime - as for most of Europe - came with the depression of the early-1930s. Unemployment rose to 2 million in 1933. The government responded by intervening more than ever in the economy, pushing up taxation considerably. Jobs were created via public works schemes; and in January 1933 the Institute for Industrial Reconstruction (IRR) was set up to provide finance for industry. Under the impetus of depression and of an aggressive foreign policy, the state - through the IRR - soon controlled 50 per cent of steel production and 80 per cent of shipbuilding. Indeed a larger share of industry was owned by the Italian state than by any other in Europe except the Soviet Union. In addition, Mussolini's government allowed certain firms - like Fiat for car manufacture and Pirelli for rubber - to achieve near monopoly status.

Output undoubtedly increased under Mussolini, with GNP growing by an average of just over one per cent per annum from 1922 to 1940, not a bad record in view of the fact that the Great Depression came in the middle of this period. In addition, the big companies were doing well and communications had dramatically improved. Furthermore there is evidence of better health among sectors of Italian society, including army recruits. But Italy was not economically self-sufficient by 1940, and - despite tax rises - there were large budget deficits. Nor was the economy ready for major war. In addition, the North-South divide was as wide as ever, and illiteracy and poverty were still major problems.

Socially, the regimentation of society definitely increased. Mussolini gave particular emphasis to youth, who were to be 'Fascistized'. In 1926 the ONB (*Opera Nazionale Balilla*) was created to indoctrinate children from 8 to 17 years old, and within a few years all children at state schools had to belong to it. There were separate sections for different age-groups, from six upwards, and also for boys and girls. The state also began publishing its own school books, glorifying Italian history and *Il Duce,* and banned the use of all others. Schoolteachers had to take an oath of loyalty to the regime from 1929, university teachers from 1931. Amongst the latter, only 11 resigned rather than accept. It is not easy to estimate the effect of such efforts, but certainly they were less than Mussolini desired. One loophole was that private and Catholic schools did not enforce ONB membership; another was that many pupils left school at the age of 11.

The *Dopolavoro* was set up in 1925 to provide leisure activities for adults. This was undoubtedly popular, and soon almost every town and village had a clubhouse. Indeed by 1939 nearly four million workers were members, including around 40 per cent of industrial workers and a quarter of peasants. But its popularity seems to have reflected not the degree to which it indoctrinated its members but the degree to which it did not. Indoctrination, its primary purpose, was generally neglected by local organisers in favour of enjoyment (in the form of sports, outings and dances).

Mussolini failed to transform the Italian people into a martial race. The history of Italy during the Second World War shows this (see page 82). Instead, he had to be content with maintaining himself in power - no mean achievement - and with magnifying or manufacturing achievements by propaganda.

b) Germany

Like Mussolini in the 1920s, Hitler in the following decade benefited from a fortunate upturn in the world economy. In the early months of 1933, when he came to power, there were the first signs of recovery. Also like the Italian, Hitler did not at first revolutionise economic policy. He too was anxious to reassure industrialists that he would do nothing to harm their interests. Hence he chose Hjalmar Schacht, head of the Reichsbank, as his financial supremo (an appointment that may be compared with that of di Stefani in Italy). Capitalists were reassured, and they applauded the improvements in the economy which were soon apparent. First priority had to be the absorption of unemployment. Government invested in construction projects, boosting electrification and autobahns, and encouraged employers to take on workers by granting tax concessions and subsidies. Well over a million more workers were taken on by the construction industries from 1933 to 1936, and industrial production doubled between 1933 and 1938. There was soon virtually full employment in Germany.

Hitler had no belief in the corporate state, but - like Mussolini - he did intervene much more in the economy. As early as February 1933 he had talked of a 'military economy' (*Wehrwirtschaft*), and in 1936 he made Hermann Göring head of the Four Year Plan, leading to Schacht's resignation the following year. Goering's brief was to prepare the armed forces and the economy for war within four years, and to this end he attempted to make Germany as self-sufficient as possible. Industry remained largely in private hands, it is true, but the free market was destroyed. The price of goods and services was decided centrally, dividends were limited and there were strict foreign exchange controls. There was also some compulsory cartelisation, so that larger enterprises could benefit from economies of scale. Germany was a state of monopolies, even more so than Italy. In addition, though the Nazis preferred to work with private enterprise, they did create their own factories if occasion demanded. For instance, the Herman Goering steelworks, set up in 1937, became the Reich's largest industrial enterprise. By 1939 a quarter of GNP was devoted to military purposes.

Germany's economic recovery was indeed substantial. But it should not be imagined that this was entirely due to Nazism. The upturn in the trade cycle was of major importance. Nor were the policies pursued with the superb efficiency portrayed by Nazi propaganda. Hitler himself often called for incompatible results: he wanted expensive new party buildings, for instance, and at the same time insisted that everything should be done to rearm. Göring once complained that Hitler was interested in how many bombers there were, but not in how many planes had engines. Nor did problems in industrial relations disappear just because the trade unions had been replaced by the DAF: after 1936, when unemployment had been largely absorbed, labour shortages encouraged workers to assert themselves, and there were go-slows, absenteeism, and even some spontaneous strikes, especially on the Ruhr. Furthermore, it should be noted that, as in Italy, economic progress was to some extent bought by sacrificing the well-being of the population. Heavy industry expanded much faster than consumer industries. R.J. Overy has calculated that the consumption of important items of food by working-class families declined considerably between 1927 and 1937: meat consumption, for example, was down by over 18 per cent, wheatbread by over 44 per cent. Furthermore, middle-class families - because of higher taxation - did not fare much better.[7] Significantly, the average working week of 43 hours had increased to 47 by 1939.

Socially, Hitler had grandiose aims. He aimed to control all aspects of Germans' lives and to create a new classless community, a *Volksgemeinschaft*. To this end he, like Mussolini, attempted to indoctrinate youth. The Hitler Youth (HJ) movement - similar to the Italian ONB - expanded rapidly so that by 1938 over 9 million boys and girls, from the ages of 10 to 18, were members. In addition, the Ministry of Education removed politically unreliable teachers and introduced changes in the curriculum to promote physical fitness and inculcate pride in German history and national identity. There was a much more thorough purge of university staff than in Italy, and in 1933-34 over 1,000 lecturers were removed from their posts, including one-third of academics in Berlin and Frankfurt. There were also special elite schools designed to produce future leaders. For the working class there was the KDF (Strength through Joy), which produced recreational provisions in similar fashion to the Italian *Dopolavoro*. Hitler also encouraged women to leave work and return to what he conceived to be their rightful roles as home-makers and mothers. He and Mussolini may have believed in the 'new man' but they had no liking for the 'new woman'. In one respect, he had no more success than Mussolini, in that the number of women in paid employment in Germany was over 10 per cent higher in 1939 than in 1933; but, on the other hand, the number of live births over the same period did rise by 50 per cent.

There was no objective social revolution in the Third Reich, since profits rose faster than wages. Insofar as there was a *Volksgemeinschaft*, it was a subjective, psychological phenomenon. In short, some Germans - we cannot be sure how many - felt that class identity ceased to matter, a belief that probably owed a great deal to the Nazi propaganda.

3 Italy and Germany: Propaganda

Many of the best writers and artists fled from Germany and Italy, and cultural life in both countries tended to be stifled. This was especially true of Nazi Germany. Hitler, who liked grandiose, allegorical or sentimental art, poured scorn on semi-abstract 'modernism'. In 1937 he even authorised a 'Degenerate Art' exhibition, whose 'hideous' exhibitions were held up to ridicule. He said that now there would be real German art once more; but not much of any value was produced. In Italy, Mussolini was less defensive than Hitler, and art was more pluralist. But he too tried to use art - and especially architecture - to glorify his regime. In short, art became the servant of propaganda.

a) Italy

Fascists made much of the assertion that, under Mussolini's super-efficient rule, the trains ran on time. The testimony of foreign visitors, however, does not bear out this assertion. Similarly guests often discovered that though taps had been fitted in the bathrooms of new hotels, sometimes these taps were not connected to any water supply. Rather than tackling Italy's fundamental problems, in fact, Mussolini devoted his energies to camouflaging their existence and projecting a glorious image of himself and his regime. He rarely missed a 'photo opportunity', and indeed - without his spectacles and shirt, with balding head totally shaved and stomach muscles tensed - he could still appear the embodiment of virile Italian manhood. An effective headline writer and phrase-maker, he spent most of each day supervising the press. Indeed all the leading Fascists in Italy were journalists. The result was an effective propaganda machine, which Goebbels was to study.

Mussolini recognised that he was living in the media age. Cheap newspapers, the radio and newsreels - together with posters - meant that there was a possibility of influencing, and perhaps even controlling, citizens as never before. Mussolini did not take all newspapers into public ownership but did insist that all should be open to government censorship, as were films, and in 1927 he took control of the radio. The number of radio licences grew from 60,000 in 1928 to almost a million 10 years later, and radio sets were given free to schools. Even so, there was only one licence for every 43 Italians, compared with one to every 7 Germans and 5 Britons. In addition, news was available from the independent Vatican Radio. Nevertheless, Mussolini was able to project an image of himself as not only supremely cultured but as prolifically athletic. Posters appeared insisting that 'Mussolini is always right' and that the primary duty of every citizen was to 'Believe, Fight and Obey'. The dynamic image of his regime was further enhanced by its style, which borrowed many of the features of D'Annunzio's short-lived dominance of Fiume.

The real secret of how to govern, said Mussolini, is to strike the imagination of the public. To his mind, governing meant not getting things done or making tangible improvements but manipulating public opinion. He was immensely proud that he could summon a cheering crowd just by pressing a bell. Indeed he was followed around by an 'applause squad' trained - with the aid of prompt cards - to cheer at the appropriate moment. The two things needed to govern Italians, he insisted, were 'policemen and bands playing in the streets'. He knew that one could usually get away with 'ninety-seven cents-worth of mere public clamour and three cents-worth of solid achievement'.[8] When Hitler paid a state visit to Rome in May 1938 Mussolini personally went over the route which the Führer's cavalcade was to take: many houses were repainted and some particularly dilapidated ones were pulled down; false trees and artificial facades were erected; and armoured cars were equipped with fine-looking wooden guns.

Almost everything was portrayed as a great success, even when no success existed. And when there were achievements of any kind (for instance, Primo Carnera became heavyweight boxing champion of the world in 1933, and Italy won the football World Cup in 1934 and 1938), they were ascribed to the beneficent impact of Fascism.

Mussolini was particularly concerned to impress foreign opinion, and many were taken in by him. After two meetings with Mussolini in January 1927, Winston Churchill told a press conference:

> Like so many others, I could not but be charmed by Signor Mussolini, and by his calm and serene manner despite so many burdens and dangers. It is easy to see that his sole thought is the lasting well-being of the Italian people as he conceives it, and that any other interest of less import has no importance in his eyes. ... If I had been an Italian I am sure I should have been entirely with you from the beginning to the end of your victorious struggle against the bestial appetites and passions of Leninism.[9]

The historian G.M. Trevelyan judged him to be 'a man of genius and ... a great man'. Yet not all were similarly enthusiastic. The novelist Ernest Hemingway, for instance, when a reporter for the *Toronto Daily Star*, was unimpressed by Mussolini, judging him to be a poseur. He wrote at the Lausanne conference in 1923:

> Mussolini is the biggest bluff in Europe. If Mussolini would have me taken out and shot tomorrow morning I would still regard him as a bluff. The shooting would be a bluff. Get hold of a good photo of Mussolini some time and study it. You will see the weakness in his mouth which forces him to scowl the famous Mussolini scowl that is imitated by every 19-year-old Fascisto in Italy. ... The Fascist dictator had announced he would receive the press. Everybody came. We all crowded into his room. Mussolini sat at his desk reading a book. His face was contorted into his famous frown. He was registering Dictator. Being an ex-newspaper man himself he knew how many readers would be reached by the accounts the men in the room would write of the interview he was about to give. And he remained absorbed in his book. Mentally he was already reading the lines of the two thousand papers served by the two hundred correspondents. 'As we entered the room the Black Shirt Dictator did not look up from the book he was reading, so intense was his concentration, etc.' I tip-toed over behind him to see what the book was he was reading with such avid interest. It was a French-English dictionary - held upside down.[10]

Another American novelist, Scott Fitzgerald, judged that anyone deceived by 'the pseudo-activity under Mussolini is deceived by the spasmodic last jerk of a corpse'. (It should, however, be recognised that Fitzgerald was arrested several times for drunkenness in Italy and bore a grudge.) Perhaps Italian Fascism was little more than a facade.

b) Germany

In March 1933 Dr Joseph Goebbels became Minister for Popular Enlightenment and Propaganda. He said his aim was 'to work on people until they are addicted to us'.[11] His methods were repetition - the biggest lie, he insisted, becomes true if repeated often enough - and a much more extensive control of the media than Mussolini had achieved. He knew that if all non-Nazi sources of information could be cut off, then the most sceptical of Germans would in time accept the Nazi message. In Hitler's Germany all the newspapers and all radio stations were controlled by the state, which also had powers of censorship over all films. In addition, Goebbels saw to it that propaganda films were widely shown.

The Nazi style of rule was in itself a powerful form of propaganda. This is seen most clearly in the large-scale rallies held each year at Nuremberg, where the whole spectacle was effectively stage-managed and choreographed. The Nazi symbols and salutes were reminiscent of a religious ceremony, and the infectious emotions of the crowds were similar to those experienced at revivalist religious meetings. Indeed several foreign journalists, of impeccable democratic credentials, found themselves momentarily taken up in the welter of emotion and almost involuntarily giving the Nazi salute.

One of the best accounts by a foreigner was given by the British writer Virginia Cowles, who was present at the 1939 rally:

> The stadium was packed with nearly 200,000 spectators. As the time for the Führer's arrival drew near, the crowd grew restless. The minutes passed and the wait seemed interminable. Suddenly the beat of the drums increased and three motor-cycles with yellow standards fluttering from their wind-shields raced through the gates. A few minutes later a fleet of black cars rolled swiftly into the arena: in one of them, standing in the front seat, his hand outstretched in the Nazi salute, was Hitler.
>
> The demonstration that followed was one of the most extraordinary I have ever witnessed. Hitler climbed to his box in the Grand Stand amid a deafening ovation, then gave a signal for the political leaders to enter. They came ... through an opening in the far end of the arena. In the silver light they seemed to pour into the bowl like a flood of water. Each of them carried a Nazi flag and when they were assembled in mass formation, the bowl looked like a shimmering sea of swastikas.
>
> Then Hitler began to speak. The crowd hushed into silence, but the drums continued their steady beat. Hitler's voice rasped into the night and every now and then the multitude broke into a roar of cheers. Some of the audience began swaying back and forth, chanting '*Sieg Heil*' over and over again in a frenzy of delirium. I looked at the faces around me and saw tears streaming down people's cheeks. The drums had grown louder and I suddenly felt frightened. For a moment I wondered if it wasn't a dream; perhaps we were really in the heart of the African jungle ...
>
> At last it was over. Hitler left the box and got back in the car. As soon as he stopped speaking the spell seemed to break and the magic vanish. That was the most extraordinary thing of all: for when he left the stand and climbed back into his car, his small figure suddenly became drab and unimpressive. You had to pinch yourself to realize that this was the man on whom the eyes of the world were riveted; that he alone held the lightning in his hands.[12]

Propaganda presented the dictators to their publics not as they really were but as they wished to appear. Consider, for instance, the two illustrations of Hitler and Mussolini below. In the absence of other images, and without personal knowledge, such depictions, repeated often, were very likely to be accepted as faithful representations of the natures of the two men.

Photo of Mussolini, 22 August 1928

Portrait of Hitler by Heinrich Knirr

4 Italy and Germany: Foreign Affairs and War

a) Italy

Voicing typical fascist rhetoric, Mussolini insisted that only blood made the wheel of history turn. In his view, war was to man as childbirth is to woman, by which he meant - not painful but - totally natural. War was something to be sought not avoided, for it would test a nation's soul. A truly Fascist foreign policy therefore meant aggressive imperial expansion.

Mussolini often insisted that he would restore the glories of the Roman Empire and make the Mediterranean 'our sea' (*Mare Nostrum*). One of his earliest actions was to bombard and occupy Corfu in 1923, after the death of Italians delimiting the Greek-Albanian border. But aggression was only one strand in his foreign policy and, for a time, not the most prominent one. He withdrew from Corfu, with compensation, under pressure from Britain; and, in 1924, he achieved his aim of annexing Fiume, but by agreement with Yugoslavia, not by force of arms. He also lavished money on a powerful chieftain and landowner in Albania, Ahmed Zog, who became king in 1928, so that Albania fell increasingly - but peacefully - under Italian influence. Furthermore he agreed, in 1925, to act as joint guarantor, with Britain, of the Franco-German border, under the terms of the Treaty of Locarno, and three years later he signed the Kellogg-Briand peace pact, as did many other nations, renouncing war as an instrument of national policy. Many believed that Mussolini, despite the bluster which made him always pose as an extremist, was settling down to become a responsible statesman.

In 1933, when the Weimar Republic ended, Mussolini felt little attraction towards Hitler and had no intention that the two 'fascist' dictators should become allies. There seemed too many sources of friction between them, stemming partly from Hitler's well-known conviction that all Germans should belong to Germany. As far back as 1922, Hitler had reassured Mussolini's emissary to Bavaria that he had no intention of claiming the Alto Adige (see page 40). But could his word be trusted? Also, whereas Hitler, the Austrian German, wanted the *Anschluss*, Mussolini looked upon Austria as his client state and sent troops to the Brenner Pass on the Italo-Austrian border when, in July 1934, an attempted coup by the Austrian nazis took place (see page 61). Mussolini was dismayed at the death of Dollfuss, a man - at only 4 feet 11 inches - for whom he felt a definite attraction. Soon afterwards he signed the Stresa Front with Britain and France, as a response to German rearmament: the three Powers let it be known that they would resist German aggression.

Hitler may have felt a high regard for Mussolini, and in *Mein Kampf* he had written of Italy as a possible ally. But in 1934 war seemed more likely than an alliance. In addition, the Fascist felt no ideological affinity with the Nazi. He dismissed *Mein Kampf* as 'a boring tome that I have never been able to read' and called Hitler's ideas 'little more than common clichés'. His ideas of racial purity and of Aryan superiority seemed nonsensical, particularly as Mussolini judged that the Germans were made up of half a dozen different races. Just after Hitler came to power, he described him as 'an ideologue who talks more than he governs ... simply a muddle-headed fellow; his brain is stuffed with philosophical and political tags that are utterly incoherent'. Nor did he think much of Göring, an 'ex-inmate of a lunatic asylum'. The two men met for the first time in 1934, and *Il Duce*, dressed in full military uniform, felt a barely disguised contempt for the German, who cut a poor figure in civilian clothes. Hitler was indeed 'a horrible sexual degenerate'![13]

Italo-German relations were at their worst in 1935. Mussolini told the Italian consul in Munich that all bridges with Germany were broken. He was about to expand his empire, and avenge the 'shameful scar' of Adowa (see page 25), by invading Abyssinia (present-day Ethiopia), a cherished project for which he had been preparing for several years. He had, he believed, secured the acquiescence of his Stresa partners, Britain and France. On the other hand, Hitler decided to send aid to the Abyssinians. But then the situation was transformed. Britain and France condemned the invasion, and at the same time Hitler reversed his policy, offering friendship - which a dangerously isolated Italy now gratefully accepted.

The new diplomatic harmony between Italy and Germany was strengthened when both states intervened in the Spanish civil war. It was Mussolini who took the lead in this venture. Hitler, around this time, posed as the respectful novice. But it was soon apparent that in fact Hitler was the head of 'Rome-Berlin Axis'. The turning point came in September 1937, when on a visit to Germany Mussolini witnessed a momentous display of power which he never forgot. In any future war, he decided, he should be with Germany, the certain victor.

Henceforth it is hard to discern much independence in Mussolini's foreign policy. In March 1938 he had to swallow the *Anschluss*, which he was not even informed about before it happened. ('When Hitler invades a country, he sends me a telegram.') Then, in September 1938, though supposedly an impartial mediator, he carried out Hitler's orders during the Munich crisis; and in May 1939 he signed the Pact of Steel, an alliance with Germany. Italian troops even adopted the German 'goose step'. Furthermore this subservience affected domestic policy. Mussolini had always mocked Hitler's racial theories and had insisted, quite correctly, that there was no Jewish problem in Italy. But from 1938 onwards - regardless of the fact that one in three adult Jews were members of the Fascist Party and that Mussolini himself had a Jewish mistress, Margherita Sarfatti - he introduced anti-Semitic legislation. State employment was denied to Jews, marriages between Jews and non-Jews were forbidden, and Jewish property was confiscated.

Even so, Mussolini showed some initiative. In April 1939 he invaded Albania and in September he refused to join the major war which Hitler had started. He had boasted earlier that if Germany mobilised at midnight, Italy would mobilise at five minutes to twelve. But, when it came to the crunch, fearful of defeat, he ignored Hitler's pleas for solidarity. He only declared war against France and Britain in June 1940 when Hitler's *Blitzkrieg* tactics had been overwhelmingly successful and when, according to all rational calculation, the war was about to be won.

In peacetime, propaganda had disguised the inefficient nature of the Fascist regime; and Mussolini hoped that in wartime it could do the same. In May 1942, for instance, he awarded the commander of an Italian submarine the highest decoration possible for sinking an American battleship. The following month the same commander was proclaimed to be a naval hero without parallel in the history of the world for sinking a second battleship. Yet, in reality, no ship of any kind had been sunk, and indeed the submarine had not even fired a torpedo in anger. There were no Italian victories in the Second World War. Mussolini was right: war did test the mettle of a regime, and it found his sadly lacking. Italy was more poorly prepared for war in 1940 than it had been in 1915.

Mussolini was the greatest boaster since Lewis Carroll's Humpty Dumpty, but his boasts were quite empty. At the end of 1940 he invaded Egypt and Greece, and in both theatres of war the Germans had to come to his rescue. Particularly glaring was the inefficiency of the home front, where Italians had to survive on very low rations. Small wonder that there was a rash of strikes in 1941. It was also clear that Mussolini was the pawn rather than the ally of Hitler. In April 1942, for instance, a meeting between the two dictators was described by an Italian observer as follows:

> Hitler talks, talks, talks, talks. Mussolini suffers - he, who is in the habit of talking himself, and who, instead, has to remain silent. On the second day, after lunch, Hitler talked uninterruptedly for an hour and forty minutes. He omitted absolutely no argument: war and peace, religion and philosophy, art and history. Mussolini automatically looked at his wrist-watch.[14]

To disguise his impotence, Mussolini insisted on choosing the announcers for the Italian radio, on drawing up the programme for the Rome opera and on deciding the exact date on which the police changed into their summer uniforms. But he scarcely knew what was really happening in Italy or in the war. A party secretary called him 'the most disobeyed man in history', and Winston Churchill aptly described him as 'the merest utensil of his master's will ... a bogus mimic of ancient Rome'.[15] If he was a Caesar, he was a 'Sawdust Caesar'. In July 1943, with the Allies in Sicily, the King and the Fascist Grand Council finally acted, placing Mussolini under arrest. He was rescued by the Germans, but his SS bodyguard were in reality his captors, and he spent the next two years as a puppet ruler in northern Italy. On 28 April 1945 he was killed by partisans.

b) Germany

Whereas Mussolini tended to be opportunistic in his ideas and in his foreign policy, Hitler had more consistent principles. He proclaimed on the first page of *Mein Kampf* that 'One blood demands one Reich'. Though willing to ignore the pocket of Germans in Italy, he did wish to see a greater Germany; and then Germany was to expand to gain 'living space' (*Lebensraum*) in the east. Believing in perpetual struggle, he undoubtedly wished to see large-scale war at some point in the future, especially against the Soviet Union. Aggression was implicit in Nazi ideology. He was also determined to control foreign policy himself and took care to dominate the decision-making process. A crisis early in 1938, whereby sexual scandals allowed him to replace Blomberg and Fritsch with his own nominees, meant that the army leadership no longer checked his actions.

The way war came about, however, was not predetermined. Insofar as major war was planned, it seems to have been intended for around 1943-45, when economic and military plans were due to mature. However, Hitler did not distinguish between diplomacy and small wars and was always prepared to seize the main chance when opportunities unexpectedly arose. In addition, he did not think that rational calculation was supremely important: what mattered in war was strength of will and the quality of dynamic leadership which he, and he alone, could provide. Having signed the Nazi-Soviet pact with Stalin in August 1939, he did not expect Britain and France to declare war, as they did early in September, when he invaded Poland: after all, without Soviet allies they would not be in a position to take any action. Hence Hitler found himself starting the Second World War without intending to. But he was not unduly concerned. He moved westwards, defeating France in June 1940. Britain then stood successfully alone but seemed in no position to do more than survive. In June 1941, therefore, Hitler went ahead with the invasion of the Soviet Union.

Germany's war effort was far more efficient than Italy's and far more brutal (though we should not forget the brutalities committed in Africa by the Italians in the 1930s, Mussolini himself ordering the extermination of whole villages). On the home front, there was a successful increase in arms production, from an index figure of 100 in January 1942 to 322 in July 1944.

Germany won a tremendous series of victories in 1939-41. She lost largely because of the superior strength of her opponents. However,

Hitler's mistakes were important - first in sending his troops into the Soviet Union without proper winter equipment and clothing, and secondly in declaring war against the United States after the Japanese attack on Pearl Harbor in December 1941. It has seemed to some commentators almost as though Hitler were determined to ensure ultimate defeat. He also made the mistake of devoting far too large a proportion of his resources to the extermination of the Jews. By 1944 the concentration camps monopolised the attention of hundreds of thousands of policemen, guards and SS and Gestapo officers. Almost certainly Hitler's anti-Semitic obsession harmed his chances of winning the war. Similarly his distrust of 'Jewish physics' led him to neglect the project to construct an Atomic bomb.

Anti-Semitism was introduced into Italy on a small scale. But in Germany and German-occupied Europe it grew into a major campaign of mass murder. Between four and six million Jews perished. There is a major historiographical debate on the Holocaust. Some believe that Hitler had, all along, intended to wage a war to the death against the Jews; others, however, judge that his ideas were far less clear-cut and that extermination emerged as 'the final solution' only during the pressures of war. There are even those who think that Hitler himself did not authorise the mass slaughter. What is certain, however, is that the Holocaust stemmed logically from the extreme and obsessive ideas which Hitler held.

Some historians - including Burleigh and Wippermann - judge that anti-Semitism is the key to understanding Nazi Germany because it was the policy to which everything else was subordinated, including foreign affairs and the conduct of the war. They argue that the primary object of the regime, its driving force, was to liquidate the 'lesser races' and thereby create a racial rather than a class society. In their view, this startling fact makes a nonsense of theories of generic fascism, for Hitler's was 'a singular regime without precedent or parallel'.[16] At any rate, there can be little doubt that the diversion of extensive resources from the war effort to exterminating Jews was illogical unless the Holocaust was accorded precedence over victory. (Sometimes, however, illogical actions are taken in war.)

Nor can there be any doubt that, by 1945, Nazism was bankrupt. Its call for perpetual struggle had led to the destruction of large areas of Germany. As many as two million German civilians and a larger number of soldiers died in the war, and it has been calculated that 90 per cent of the buildings in Germany's major cities had been damaged or destroyed by Allied bombing. Most Germans did stand by Hitler, in bad times as well as good, but his regime had crumbled. Hitler's fate embodied the unwisdom of relying on one man. He proved no superman: indeed all along he had been human - all too human. Hitler, who had once boasted of being the hardest man the German nation had produced in generations, and perhaps in centuries, was now increasingly feeble. By the beginning of 1945 the strain had begun to tell and he had passed largely into a world of fantasy, reinforced by the unwillingness of his aides to tell him the truth about the war. After Stalingrad, where the Germans were defeated in January 1943, he found it difficult ever to relax: 'I keep seeing the staff maps in the dark, and my brain goes grinding on and on. It takes me hours to get to sleep. If I put out the light, I can sketch where every division was at Stalingrad. It goes on for hours till I get to sleep at five or six.'[17] He committed suicide in April 1945.

5 Other Regimes

The so-called Fatherland Front, set up by Dollfuss in Austria, was little more than a facade: the capitalist practices which the corporate state was supposed to eliminate flourished. But in fact the 'Austrofascists' (see page 61) were in power for too short a time to achieve much. The regimes set up by the Nazis during the war - for instance, in Vichy France and in Romania - are excluded from this discussion because they were largely imposed from without and cannot be said to represent authentic local regimes. Aside from Italy and Germany, therefore, attention must centre only on Franco's Spain, and the degree to which this was fascist is open to doubt (see page 50).

a) Spain

On several counts, the similarity between Franco's Spain and Fascist Italy and Nazi Germany is remarkable. Franco was an anti-Marxist, like the Italian and German leaders, and he too banned trade unions. He was also anti-liberal, banning all political parties. Indeed he shared many of the 'anti' characteristics of the fascists. Also, he was definitely a dictator, amassing considerable power in his own hands. The master of Spain by 1 April 1939, when the civil war came to an end, he later made himself regent for life - without any king being on the throne! He alone appointed and dismissed ministers and decided government policy - and he did so until his death in 1975. As in Italy and Germany, there was a cult of personality around the leader - in this case known as the *Caudillo* - and images of the great national hero, who was said to have saved Spain from the red menace, were to be seen almost everywhere.

In other ways too the Franco regime seems to qualify as fascist. Franco set up a Labour Organisation, which may be compared to the DAF in Germany. He also constructed a corporate state on Italian lines: that is to say that a corporate state, as in Italy, existed on paper though not in reality. Furthermore he controlled the contents of education and inaugurated a youth movement to indoctrinate the young. There was a good deal of censorship in Spain. Finally, Franco was also very harsh on his enemies. After victory in the civil war, thousands of his opponents were executed, thousands were imprisoned and tens of thousands were forced into exile. It was said that the word 'pity' had been struck from the Spanish dictionary.

Add to these factors the fact that Franco, as a soldier, was obviously a militarist, and it may seem that he qualifies as a fascist. Minor differences from the Italian or German models may surely be explained by pointing out that the nationalist component in fascism inevitably produces some national variations. And yet the case is far from proven.

First, it must be conceded that Franco was a very different sort of man from Hitler or Mussolini. They were first and foremost politicians, but he was pre-eminently a soldier, and a successful one. He had entered an officers' academy at the age of 14 and worked his way up, becoming the youngest general in Europe in 1926, at the age of 33. He was never a member of any political party, and thus there was no equivalent of the Nazis or the Fascists in Spain. The Falange, as we have seen, was the nearest Spain came to possessing a fascist party, but Franco took actions to limit its importance (see page 50) - and members of the Falange responded in 1940 with an assassination attempt. Franco also lacked charisma, being a reserved and serious loner incapable of making effectively emotional speeches. Also he formed a genuine alliance with the church, rather than the cynical concordats of Mussolini and Hitler. Certainly, as a real believer, he had no wish to create any new secular religion. Catholicism thus provided the basic ideology of his regime, not new-fangled fascism. Hitler described his followers, distastefully, as 'clerico-monarchical scum'.[18] Certainly Franco had no wish to create a 'new man': he simply wanted to return to the good old days, and his ideal was the past greatness of his hero Philip II. Many have described the atmosphere of his rule as old-fashioned, dull and repressive, as more feudal than fascist.

Nor, unlike Hitler and Mussolini, did Franco follow an aggressive foreign policy. Perhaps he simply had no taste for overseas adventures, or perhaps he realised that the fragile Spanish economy could not survive a major foreign war. Admittedly he had joined the Anti-Comintern Pact (with Germany, Italy and Japan) as soon as the civil war was over, and had then left the League of Nations. But when the Second World War started he, along with Salazar in Portugal, declared Iberian neutrality; and even when Italy joined the conflict and France fell, he would go no further than 'non-belligerence', providing Hitler with strategic and material support. As many as 20,000 Spanish troops fought with German forces in the Soviet Union, but these were all volunteers, mostly Falangists. In October 1940, meeting with Hitler in Spain, Franco spoke of the possibility of full participation but, at the same time, laid down unacceptable conditions. Hitler tried to overawe him, but without any success. Indeed the Führer found the Spanish leader implacable. After a conversation lasting nine hours, Hitler gave up, later telling Mussolini that rather than go through that again 'he would prefer to have three or four teeth taken out'.[19]

The cartoon below is therefore a very poor and inadequate representation of Franco. The Spanish leader is presented as a rather pathetic midget, hiding meekly behind Hitler and Mussolini, so that his very existence seemed to be in doubt. This may have been the impression he tried to give - especially to the dictators on whose military aid he was relying in the civil war: Mussolini alone contributed 50,000 troops, 950 tanks, 760 aeroplanes and 91 warships to the Nationalist cause. It was also an understandable error when the cartoon was published, in 1937. But it was hardly the truth. He seemed to be a pawn in the hands of Hitler and Mussolini, whereas the exact opposite may be closer to reality.

Many who opposed Franco believed that they were fighting 'against fascism'. The truth, however, was far more complicated than they knew; and many modern historians describe Franco's Spain as much closer to a military dictatorship than a fascist state. In 1938-45, for instance, half of all ministerial appointments were held by senior military men. Yet of course much depends whether we adopt a 'hard' or 'soft' definition of fascism.

The Question of Franco's Existence, Evening Standard, *28 July 1937*

6 Assessment

Fascism can be assessed in two ways. First, it can be analysed in terms of ideas and ideologies (as, for instance, on pages 9-10). This is the method of the philosopher or historian of ideas, and it is perfectly legitimate (though it carries the danger that we may end up assigning more importance to theory than practice). Secondly, 'fascism' can be interpreted, in a common-sense way, as signifying the regimes which either called themselves or have been widely called 'fascist'. According to this view, the term is a shorthand for the sorts of policies undertaken in states like Italy and Germany, and for the rationale or propaganda that accompanied and justified them. This method does not seek to construct some ideal model - or essence - of fascism, against which regimes can then be measured. On the contrary, it accepts that words are defined only by the ways in which they are used: and if, for instance, enough people have called Franco's Spain a fascist state, it accepts this usage.

On the other hand, it is useful to judge how similar - or homogeneous - the so-called fascist regimes were. If the differences outweigh the similarities, we cannot say that the common fascist label must not be applied to them (after all, no one will take any notice!), but we can decide whether the term *should* be used. Certainly this approach will help us judge how useful the term is and whether it implies a vague or specific meaning.

Several questions prompted by the material in this chapter can be considered using this common-sense viewpoint:

1) Do Italy and Germany have enough in common to warrant the single label 'fascist'? Certainly they have undoubted similarities, in terms of political, social and economic policies, and in terms of the propaganda techniques used to indoctrinate the masses. But we often in history (as in life) do find what we are looking for simply because we are looking for it. Hence we must also seek for differences, and indeed we can find these as well. Fascism and Nazism did perform very differently, especially during the Second World War, and did at times pursue contrasting policies, as towards the Jews. Hitler was obviously far more racist and also expansionist than Mussolini, and his regime was far more intolerant and efficient. The issue, therefore, is the balance that should be struck between similarities and differences - and, history and historians being what they are, no two students of history will be likely to strike exactly the same balance.

The relationship between Fascism and Nazism is extremely complex, like that between Hitler and Mussolini. Mussolini began by having contempt for Hitler and treated him accordingly. Then, realising the extent of Nazi power, he treated Hitter with subservience, though still retaining a now unspoken contempt. Hitler, on the other hand, began by treating Mussolini with respect but then veered towards condescension, while still in fact retaining an unrealistic admiration for him. Hence there was no identity between the two men, or between their regimes, and in some ways they were different. Many discern some sort of family relationship between them which justifies the common 'fascist' label. But, if this is true, it does mean that the word carries a highly flexible meaning.

2) Should only Italy and Germany be called fascist? In particular, should Spain under Franco? This regime was created, above all, by the army not a fascist party, and it was buttressed by Catholicism rather than by any particularly fascist ideology. If, therefore, the regime is called fascist, the term can only be used not merely flexibly but in the weakest and most general sense, signifying non-communist authoritarianism. Some consider that the regime should not be considered fascist at all. But the fact is that it is often labelled in this way. Perhaps, therefore, Franco's regime should be considered as a sub-division or even as a variation of fascism. Or perhaps the word is relevant only to particular aspects of the whole regime, like its anti-communism, its contempt for democracy and its repression.

References

1 Denis Mack Smith, *Mussolini* (Granada, 1983), p. 218; S.J. Woolf (ed), *European Fascism* (Weidenfeld and Nicolson, 1968), p. 44.
2 S.G. Payne, *A History of Fascism* (UCL Press, 1995) p. 117.
3 David Welch, *Modern European History, 1871-1975: A Documentary Reader* (Heinemann, 1994), p. 140; Roger Eatwell, *Fascism: A History* (Chatto, 1995), p. 113.
4 William Carr, *Hitler* (Edward Arnold, 1978), p. 41.
5 Payne, *History of Fascism,* p. 117.
6 Philip Morgan, *Italian Fascism* (Macmillan, 1995), pp. 97-8.
7 R.J. Overy, *The Nazi Economic Recovery, 1932-38* (Macmillan, 1982).
8 Mack Smith, *Mussolini,* pp. 205, 171.
9 R.R. James (ed), *Churchill Speaks* (Windward, 1980), p. 489.
10 Ernest Hemingway, *By-Line: Selected Articles and Dispatches of Four Decades* (Grafton Books, 1968), pp. 84-6.
11 Welch, *Modern European History,* p. 126.
12 Virginia Cowles, *Looking for Trouble* (Hamish Hamilton, 1941), pp. 153-4.
13 Mack Smith, *Mussolini,* pp. 200, 212-15.
14 Malcolm Muggeridge (ed), *Ciano's Diary, 1939-1943,* 29 April 1942, (Heinemann, 1947), p. 250.
15 Mack Smith, *Mussolini,* p. 327; James (ed), *Churchill Speaks,* p. 783.
16 Michael Burleigh and Wolfgang Wippermann, *The Racial State: Germany 1933-1945* (CUP, 1991), p. 307.
17 Norman Stone, *Hitler* (Coronet, 1982), p. 201.
18 Mark Robson, *Italy: Liberalism and Fascism 1870-1945* (Hodder and Stoughton, 1992), p. 92.
19 Alan Bullock, *Hitler: A Study in Tyranny* (Penguin, 1962), p. 605.

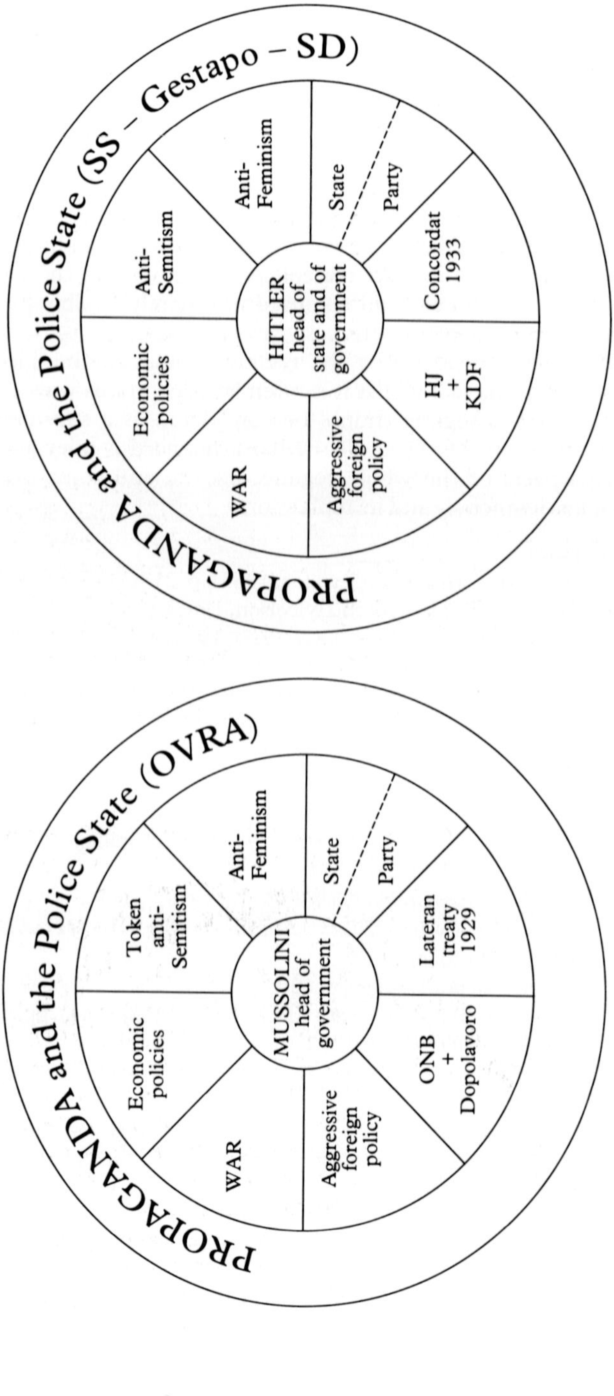

Summary - Fascism in Action

Answering essay questions on *'Fascism in Action'*

Questions on this issue are extremely popular. Consider the following examples:

1 What were the chief characteristics, in both theory and practice, of Fascism in Italy and Nazism in Germany?
2 What were the basic principles of Italian Fascism and German Nazism?
3 Discuss the view that the regime of Mussolini was less oppressive than that of Hitler.
4 How great were the similarities between the regimes of Mussolini, Hitler and Franco?
5 'Hitler was a fascist who sometimes posed as a conservative; Franco was a conservative who sometimes posed as a fascist.' Discuss this statement.

All essays should have a beginning, a middle and an end; but all too often (as Philip Larkin said of modern novels) they have a beginning, a *muddle* and an end. Hence it is worth thinking about the important middle paragraphs and constructing plans for the above titles. The important thing to grasp is that each middle paragraph should focus on one sub-division, or relevant theme, of your answer (which should be signposted briefly in the opening paragraph). Deal with one issue thoroughly, and do not return to it later on for a second bite of the cherry. Particularly important issues can be spread over several paragraphs, but do not include several separate issues in the same paragraph. What issues warrant a paragraph each for the first title? Presumably you will include a section on the form which dictatorship took in the two states (a broad topic which might well warrant several paragraphs), on economic organisation, social regimentation and on foreign policy. (Of course your choice will depend partly on your knowledge: give whole paragraphs to the topics you are knowledgeable about, so long as they are relevant; otherwise you may have to content yourself with a sentence or two tagged on to other paragraphs.) Remember that the question asks about the 'chief' characteristics of the regimes, so do not try to include everything. Will you give propaganda a separate paragraph? Perhaps propaganda can be related to the 'theory' part of the question: propaganda showed what 'in theory', though not in reality, the regimes were about. You should at least consider looking at theory and reality in every middle paragraph, rather than having separate sections on each.

Always make sure that in every middle paragraph you have a judicious blend of generalisation and detail. Never just give general statements (arguments) and never have a whole paragraph full of nothing but details (evidence). You must have both. Why not start each middle paragraph with an argument, relevant to a sub-division of question set, and then bring forward the best evidence to try to prove it. (You never will actually prove it, but you can certainly support it and make it seem logical.)

It is implicit in this advice that the whole essay should answer the question directly. You should not just narrate and describe in your middle paragraphs and then, in the final paragraph, answer the question. Hence you must have your overall interpretation worked out before you start the middle paragraphs, and these paragraphs should be written to support that interpretation. (Think of yourself as a barrister arguing a case, not as a novelist telling a story.) In this way you will avoid giving narrative and being irrelevant, and you will - almost automatically - construct the sort of logical argument which gets good marks.

Try drawing up lists of middle paragraphs for questions 2-5. (Remember that for question 2, on fascist principles, you will need to refer to material in chapters 2 and 3, as well as in this chapter.) Then you might compose first sentences - consisting of suitable generalisations - for each of these. Finally, you should complete sample paragraphs by adding well-chosen details as evidence - and remember that historians' opinions are only opinions, not the hard evidence you need. As a general rule, quote the evidence the historians quote rather than the historians themselves.

Source-based questions on 'Fascism in Action'

1 Two views of Mussolini

Read the extracts from Churchill and Hemingway on pages 76 and 77. Answer the following questions:

a) Assess from his words how important anti-Leninism was in Churchill's evaluation of Mussolini. (3 marks)
b) Does Churchill appear at all credulous or naive in this extract? (3 marks)
c) How may Hemingway's own character and motives have influenced this estimate of Mussolini? (5 marks)
d) Do you find Churchill's or Hemingway's account the more useful? Explain your answer. (4 marks)
e) How may the circumstances of the time in which the extracts were written have affected the views of the authors? (5 marks)

2 Two Images of the Dictators

Study the photograph of Mussolini and the portrait of Hitler on page 79. Answer the following questions:

a) Sum up the general image that was portrayed of each dictator. (3 marks)

b) What are the main differences and the main similarities between the two images? (3 marks)
c) Explain how each image has been constructed. Pay particular attention to the facial expression, the clothing and the poses of the two men, as well as to the background against which they are presented and to the 'angle of vision' from which they are seen. (10 marks)
d) Were these images of Mussolini and Hitler particularly suitable for 1928 and 1937 respectively? (4 marks)

Hints and Advice: It is essential not to rush the analysis of visual sources. No one jumps in feet first with written texts, if only because it takes time to read them; but we are able to take in illustrations at a glance, and so people are inclined to form conclusions too quickly. Remember that conclusions should come at the end of study not at the beginning; and it is good advice to make a conscious effort to go slowly when analysing visual material. Paintings, photographs and cartoons invariably contain more than we imagine, so scrutinise each illustration carefully and thoroughly. Also, read all the questions before attempting the first: otherwise you could include in your answer to (a) material best reserved for (b)-(d).

How will you tackle (a)? Remember that the question asks about the image 'that was portrayed', and so you must concentrate on how people at the time would have perceived them. (Today, we may perceive them very differently, because we have different values and have had different experiences.) Try to sum up the essence of the two illustrations, without going into too much detail. After all, there are only 3 marks at stake. The youthful dynamism and heroism of Mussolini is easy to spot, but it is not so easy to sum up this version of Hitler. If you have real difficulty, you could come back to this question after tackling the others. Certainly it is a good idea to make sure that your answers complement each other.

For (b), the differences are easy to spot, but what about the similarities? Are both men portrayed as being serious, dedicated leaders? Could the adjective 'dignified' be applied to them? Is each leader 'centre-stage', so to speak? (Don't neglect the obvious! Simple points, so long as they are relevant, will score marks.)

There are 10 marks available for (c), so you must give particular prominence to this question. Fortunately you are given a check-list, so go through each component carefully. It will probably be best to have brief paragraphs on each item in the check list, bringing in evidence from both of the illustrations, though you could tackle each dictator in separate parts of your answer. (Why not try each approach until you see from experience which way is better?) Note how each aspect of the image reinforces all the others and helps to create the 'meaning' of the illustration. For instance, the splendid military uniform of Mussolini complements his dramatic gesture and the impassioned expression on his face, an effect heightened by the Blackshirts and the imposing facade of the building. What do you think is the effect of the camera-angle? Probably the more we look up to a person - literally - the more we may be inclined to look up to him (or venerate him) figuratively. We seem to be closer to Hitler - he seems nearer to the surface of the canvas (or the 'picture plane'), a fact that emphasises his dependable, respectable, middle-aged, Uncle-like image; but we are still looking up to him. In no sense can we aspire to be his equals. Note that the question asks us to pay particular attention to certain features of the illustrations: this means that we are free to bring in other features. Can you think of any?

Question (d) asks us to 'contextualise' the illustrations. You must bring your existing knowledge to bear. What is happening in Italy and Germany around 1928 and 1937? Did Mussolini always try to convey an image of dynamism? Was the conservative, rural image of Hitler particularly apt for 1937, when he wished to distance himself from the radicalism of the SA and perhaps to appeal especially to the traditional members of the military establishment?

CHAPTER 5

The Significance of Fascism

1 Fascism, Capitalism and Class

a) The Orthodox Communist View

At a meeting of the Comintern (an international communist organisation set up by Lenin) in December 1933, leading Marxist intellectuals gave a definition of fascism which stressed its close connections with capitalism. In their view, fascism was 'the open terrorist dictatorship of the most reactionary, most chauvinist and most imperialistic elements of finance capital'.[1] World history, they believed, followed a definite path: feudalism had given way to capitalism, which, in its turn, was sure to give way eventually to communism, after an uprising by the proletariat. In their view, however, the capitalists would do all in their power to prevent this happening - and hence they had brought about fascism in countries ripe for revolution. Fascism was therefore the last stage of capitalism, in which the owners of the means of production vainly used dictatorship and terrorism to oppress the workers and stave off the inevitable revolution.

Very few people would today accept this theory in its entirety. After all, events proved it incorrect. Fascism was defeated in 1945, but this did not usher in communism, except where the Red Army overran eastern Europe. On the contrary, capitalism flourished after the Second World War, making a nonsense of Marxist predictions. But can we accept any elements of the theory? Are there important links between fascism and capitalism? We have seen in the previous chapters that there are.

Mussolini's rise to power was certainly aided by capitalists. It was the Perone brothers, arms manufacturers in Milan, and others who helped finance *Il Popolo d'Italia*, and their support also saved the Fascists from oblivion during the *Biennio rosso*. In addition, we have seen that fear of communism was a major factor in Mussolini's rise to power. Similarly, *Il Duce* was at pains to dissociate himself from Fascist radicalism or socialism, and (with help from di Stefani) he initially lowered taxes, banned strikes and followed other policies designed to win the support of big business. Even when he abandoned *laissez faire* in efforts to make the economy self-sufficient, Mussolini pursed policies favourable to large capitalist firms like Fiat and Pirelli.

It was a similar story in Germany. Anti-communism helped Hitler's rise to power, and he was supported by several powerful capitalists. For instance, the media tycoon Alfred Hugenberg helped him from the late-1920s. Hitler gained respectability by association with such figures, and soon donations to the party were forthcoming from industrialists like Emil Kirdorf and Fritz Thyssen, the coal and steel magnates. Also like Mussolini, Hitler soon dissociated himself from the radical wing of his party. He also (with the help of Schacht) at first reassured the capitalists; and then, despite the drive towards autarcky, leading firms like I.G. Farben still flourished. Indeed capitalist profits were higher than ever before in 1940, and there seemed to be a cosy, symbiotic relationship between capitalism and Nazism.

Perhaps, therefore, there is some validity in the Marxist view of fascism. Yet we must be careful not to exaggerate the influence of the leading capitalist figures. They may have aided the rise of fascism, but - as we saw in chapter 3 - they were hardly solely responsible for it. Admittedly industrialists often gave donations to fascist parties, but they did so as a kind of insurance - in case they ever came to power; and nor was such money distributed solely to fascist groups. Most industrialists were in fact almost certainly hostile to the Nazi party in 1929-32, and it was only after Hitler became Chancellor that money began to pour in. For instance, at a meeting on 20 February 1933 Hitler was promised three million Reichsmarks from 20 industrialists: these were in the nature of 'sweeteners', to ensure that government policy was favourable to big business. Before that, the party had been largely self-financing. Even after 1933 some industrialists - especially those who manufactured for export and so favoured free trade - were less favourable to the regime than others. Certainly we must avoid the temptation to suppose that those who made donations could control the dictators, however much they may have hoped to do so. The profits of many industrialists - especially arms manufacturers - may well have soared in the late-1930s in Germany and Italy, but this does not mean that the dictators danced to their tune. On the contrary, it probably makes more sense to see the dictators as the puppeteers rather than the puppets. Thyssen, who had been pleased to see Hitler in power in 1933, actually fled the country in 1939, insisting that the Nazis were little better than the Soviets. Whereas Marxists tend to believe that economics determine politics, Hitler judged that, on the contrary, the opposite was the case: those with political power determine economic policies. It was Hitler himself who made the key decisions which launched a world war; the industrialists had no influence whatever on German foreign policy during the war; and by 1945 the country's capitalist economy had been devastated.

b) Class: Who were the Fascists?

According to the another left-wing interpretation, mass support for the fascists came overwhelmingly from a single group, the petty bourgeoisie (the lower middle class), which feared loss of status and descent into the realms of the proletariat ('proletarianisation'). According to this theory, fascism was the extremism of the middle class, just as liberalism was its moderate political stance (and similarly communism and social democracy were the extreme and moderate ideologies of the working class). If support for Fascism and Nazism did come largely from a single sector, rather than from a general cross-section of society, then this may provide a key to understanding its nature.

An investigation of this issue must centre not on the later stages of fascism - when the parties were mass organisations and party membership was a passport to advancement - but on the earlier stages, when those who were truly committed joined fascist movements.

Detailed evidence on the composition of the Fascist Party survives for November 1921, the month after its formation, and this may be compared with information from the Italian census of the same year. Members of the party included 24,000 professionals, 32,000 landowners and greater numbers of peasants and industrial workers. If these figures are correct, it seems that though the leadership was overwhelmingly middle-class (as one might expect with any political party - even Lenin's Bolshevik party in Russia), the party itself was not far off being a cross-section of Italian society. Workers (industrial and agricultural) comprised 24.3 per cent of the party and 21.8 per cent of the population as a whole. The middle classes made up 56.5 per cent of the party and 53.5 per cent of society as a whole. In addition, industrialists comprised 2.8 per cent of the party and 1.7 per cent of the population. The deviation between party and nation is thus remarkably small. The only group to be significantly over-represented in Fascist ranks were students, 13 per cent of whom joined the party. Indeed youth as a whole was over-represented. This should not surprise us, given that the Fascists projected themselves of the party of youth.

For Germany the issue may be investigated by assessing election figures for May 1928, September 1930 and July 1932 (the three fairest elections in which the Nazis took part). Who voted Nazi? Was the party a *Klassenpartei*, drawing its support mainly from one class, or a *Volkspartei*, gaining support from all sections of society? In 1928 the Nazis won only 2.5 per cent (800,000) of the total votes. Most of these were gained in rural areas, especially in the north-west of the country. What this showed was not that a single class but that those parts of the population undergoing economic depression were particularly receptive to the Nazi message. At the next election, in September 1930, therefore - amidst widespread national depression - the party could expect to appeal to a larger number, and they did so, polling 6.4 million votes, 18 per cent of the total. The combined votes of the left-wing parties, the SPD and the KPD, increased, communists picking up votes from the social democrats; and support also rose a little for the Catholic Centre party. Therefore the Nazis must have taken votes from the largely middle-class liberal parties and from other right-wing parties. In fact the vote of the Nationalists fell by more than half. In addition, many who had not bothered to vote at the previous poll probably supported them, in a larger turn-out, as did many first-time voters. In July 1932 these trends continued. The Nazi vote peaked at 13.7 million, 37 per cent of the total. The combined SDP-KPD vote was virtually static and the

Centre party lost only 500,000 votes - and therefore it seems certain that the Nazis gained votes from the other parties and from those who had just become eligible to vote.

These statistics are open to a variety of interpretations, and - given that the ballot was secret - we should not be too dogmatic in our views. But it does seem that Catholics and industrial workers were relatively immune to Nazi propaganda. This is confirmed by an examination of the results for particular districts. The Nazis did better in the north and the east than in the south and the west, better among rural than urban communities. Their vote was higher in small towns than in large cities. It is highly likely, therefore, that the middle classes - especially members of the old lower middle class (shopkeepers, small farmers, craftsmen, handicraft workers and civil servants) - were probably over-represented among Nazi voters. There were working-class Nazi voters but they seem to have been under-represented. Probably only around a quarter of workers voted Nazi.

Does this mean that the Nazi party was a *Klassenpartei*? Some have argued that it was, but it should be borne in mind that detailed research has revealed a number of cleavages among the electorate. Protestants were more likely to vote Nazi than Catholics, the young rather than the old, and women rather than men - and all such divisions cannot be fully explained by a class analysis. There are also exceptions to the broad regional pattern of Nazi support which nothing seems to explain adequately. Furthermore it has been calculated that almost a third of Nazi party *members* at this time were working-class. This was less than in the population as a whole, but it was still a very significant number, and workers were well represented in the SA. It does seem therefore that although the party was not a *Volkspartei* at this time (how could it be when only 37 per cent of the population voted Nazi?), it was more of a genuine people's party than other political organisations, which were focused towards particular interest groups. Or at least it was during the July 1932 election: the Nazi vote fell later that year. It also seems that the Marxist view of fascism as a movement of the petty bourgeoisie is inadequate: fascism is a more wide-ranging phenomenon than the communist view allows. Nor - it must be added - does the class-based interpretation provide a sufficient explanation of how Hitler achieved real political power.

The Nazi party, like the Fascist party, was so successful partly because it could appeal to different groups of people for different - even contradictory - reasons. Class identity was probably one factor in the rise of fascism, but it was certainly not the only one. Other factors were important in motivating support, including the force of nationalism, which transcended class allegiance. Also important was the charisma of the leader and the character-type of those converted - and sometimes the commitment to Nazism was like a religious conversion. 'I cannot go back,' a German explained after meeting Hitler for the first time, 'I cannot question, I am pledged. ... I am as much committed to Hitler as the fundamentalist is to his Bible'.[2] This sort of commitment requires a psychological, rather than a solely economic or class-based, explanation.

2 Fascism: Revolutionary or Reactionary?

One key question about fascism is whether it was a revolutionary or a reactionary force. In other words, did it produce momentous change, perhaps even modernising the countries affected by it? Or, on the contrary, did it try to put the clock back and prevent modernisation?

Much ink has been spent on this question, but without any clear consensus emerging. This should not surprise us, for several reasons. First, much depends on the definitions adopted. Some define fascism as a revolutionary, modernising force - and then proceed to select suitable evidence to support this view, often stopping short of the mass war of destruction that took place between 1940 and 1945. In addition, 'modernisation' has no agreed definition. Most people equate this process, in general terms, with industrialisation, urbanisation and - perhaps - secularisation, but the whole issue is highly problematic. Is feminism 'modern'? If so, fascism's stress on the traditional (home-maker) image of woman may seem old-fashioned and reactionary. What about genocide and total war? Should these be considered modern? One hopes that they are not characteristic features of the modern world but perhaps they are, and certainly they did not occur before the twentieth century. There is also the problem of whether we judge fascist regimes by their intention or their achievement - for example, by their anti-feminist rhetoric or by the fact that more women worked outside the home in Fascist Italy and Nazi Germany. And should we judge the regimes by their short-term or long-term effects? If the latter, then perhaps even the mass destruction wrought by the Second World War on Germany should be considered as modernising, in that after the war the country had to be rebuilt almost from scratch and so could utilise the latest industrial machinery. If so, then the fascists were largely unwitting modernisers. Another problematic issue is whether the modernisation promoted during the periods of fascist rule was, in fact, promoted by fascism. In short, would it have occurred anyway, regardless of who was in power?

There is also the issue of whether the fascist regimes were a complete change from what preceded them - in which case they may definitely be considered revolutionary - or whether they built upon the pre-fascist periods. This is a highly controversial issue, especially in the case of Nazi Germany, and also a highly complex one. Simple explanations will not do: we have to recognise that the fascist regimes built on the legacy of the past but also introduced important changes.

The fact is that the fascist regimes appeared, at different times and from different perspectives, as revolutionary and as reactionary and also as conservative. A single label surely distorts a complex reality. Nor should we ignore the fact that there were important differences between the so-called fascist states. Mussolini's regime, for instance, was less revolutionary than Hitler's. Mussolini liked the associations of the word 'revolutionary' and insisted that it applied to his regime: indeed Fascism, he said, meant 'permanent revolution'. On the other hand, he also liked to call it a 'restoration', a revival of past associations.[3] He did foster important changes, but on the whole Fascist propaganda and the cult of the Duce were substitutes for modernisation. Hitler's achievement too was partly bogus. Just as the corporate state did not exist in Italy, so in Germany a *Volksgemeinschaft* was never fully realised. Yet few can doubt that the Nazi regime was stronger than the Fascist or that its achievements had greater effects on its citizens.

3 Fascism and Totalitarianism

Another explanation for the nature of fascism has been put forward by those who argue that the fascist regimes were totalitarian. One problem with this view is the difficulty of defining this term. There has in fact been a debate - similar to that about fascism - over exactly which qualities a regime must exhibit before it should be called totalitarian. A common-sense viewpoint, however, is that a fully totalitarian government controls the whole life of its citizens. (Thus *everything* should be rendered unto Caesar.) Mussolini used the term in October 1925 about his rule in Italy: it signified 'everything within the state, nothing outside the state, nothing against the state'.[4] Similarly Goebbels insisted in November 1933 that the Nazi regime must be 'a totalitarian state pervading all spheres' of life.[5] But if the leaders of Fascist Italy and Nazi Germany had the same broad goals, we still have to ask whether they achieved them. We also have to ask whether other states - and in particular the Soviet Union - had the same broad characteristics.

In George Orwell's *Nineteen Eighty-Four* the tyrannical regime in Oceania utilised the Thought Police, and television screens that spied on their viewers, to root out dissidents. It thus seemed as though Big Brother was always watching you. In addition, there was incessant propaganda designed to control the perceptions of the public: even history was constantly being re-written to fit in with the current party line. Hence, if the party so decided, two and two equalled five. The hero of the book, Winston Smith, imagined at first that at least the few cubic centimetres inside his skull were his own. By the end of the book, however, even this last bastion had been eliminated: he loved Big Brother. But of course such total control existed only in the realms of fiction. In reality it was impossible to control every aspect of life. Hence we must ask the degree to which Mussolini and Hitler achieved their totalitarian aims.

We have seen that Mussolini's regime was built on a facade. He called his rule totalitarian, but it was not. After all, the king was still head of state; the state and the party each co-existed; the armed forces had considerable autonomy; and the church had some independence, as did cultural life. As Stanley Payne has written, 'Mussolini came to power on the basis of a tacit compromise with established institutions, and he was never able fully to escape the constraints of that compromise.'[6] There was certainly acceptance of the regime by the mass of Italians, but not much love for it - and during the Second World War it was extremely unpopular. Many Italians conformed outwardly, but their spirit was untouched - at least this was Mussolini's complaint. Traditional values survived.

Was this also the case in Germany? Here the regime was much more efficient. Terror, for instance, was practised on a much larger scale. Yet the administration of the Third Reich was also comparatively chaotic, with overlapping jurisdictions between various organisations; and the continued existence of private enterprise meant that the economy was never fully controlled by the government. Hence the word totalitarian cannot be accepted without qualification. Furthermore research in particular German localities - i.e. 'from the bottom up' - indicates that the hold of the Nazi regime on the hearts and minds of the German people was not complete. There were definite traces of dissent, even though Hitler personally was very popular. In addition, there was also some outright opposition. This can be seen not only in the isolated attempts to assassinate Hitler (for instance that by Stauffenberg in July 1944) but in conflict between church and state. Hitler may have signed a concordat with the papacy in 1933, but many Nazis hated the church, and Hitler privately believed that one could not be a Christian and a Nazi. Many church leaders accepted the logic of this view, and they particularly disapproved of the project to produce a 'racially-pure' German state. When in 1939-41, as part of its euthanasia programme, the government removed about 70,00 people from mental institutions and killed them, Catholics and Protestants complained. In the end - uniquely - the Nazis backed down, good evidence that the regime did not completely control all the Germans all the time.

The other key issue is the degree of identity between the fascist powers and the Soviet Union. During the Cold War (the period of acute international tension between the West and the USSR after the Second World War) it became commonplace for western historians to brand the old fascist enemy and the new communist enemy with the common totalitarian label. More recently, however, such reasoning has been dismissed as Cold War propaganda. But should the fascists and the communists be described in this way? The question is well worth asking. What did they have in common?

Orwell certainly had Italy, Germany and the USSR in mind when he wrote *Nineteen Eighty-Four*, and with good reasons. Each regime was a repressive police state: the SS and the OVRA were paralleled in the

Soviet Union by the NKVD. In all of them citizens were exposed to brutality, indoctrination and regimentation. In all of them too the state directed the economy to some degree, though this took the form of state ownership in Russia. They were also personal dictatorships. Mussolini tamed the *Ras*, Hitler the SA; and in the show trials of the 1930s Stalin showed that his control of the Bolshevik party was complete. All three were therefore above party. There may have been different degrees of totalitarianism in each, but the broad similarities are obvious. Small wonder that Mussolini insisted that Lenin, like himself, was an artist who worked in people, as other artists used marble, or that in the late-1930s he referred to Stalin as a crypto-fascist. In particular they used similar propaganda techniques. See, for instance, the poster of Stalin below (which may be compared with those of the fascist dictators on page 79): he bestrides the world like a colossus. This could quite easily, with minor changes, be an example of fascist propaganda.

Fascism under Mussolini and Hitler and communism under Stalin obviously had far more in common than either side cared to admit. Yet they are generally placed at opposite ends of the political spectrum, the former on the extreme right and the latter on the extreme left. This is largely because of their ideological differences. Communism purported to be a movement of the working class, with the internationalist aim of

A poster showing Stalin

fomenting world revolution, fascism to be a nationalist movement bridging class divisions. Certainly there are differences here. But how important are they? Much obviously depends on how important ideology was in practice. Were the dictators sincere in their principles? It is at least arguable that principles were much less important to them than power. When Stalin arraigned the Old Bolsheviks on trumped-up charges and subsequently executed them, did he not forgo all intellectual respectability? Perhaps power was not obtained to serve ideology: ideology may have been simply a means of legitimising power. This was certainly Orwell's view: 'One does not establish a dictatorship in order to safeguard a revolution; one makes a revolution in order to establish the dictatorship. The object of persecution is persecution. The object of torture is torture. The object of power is power.'[7] Were the dictators ideologically opportunistic? They may have been unprincipled in their tactics, but were they in their ultimate aims? The rest of the chapter examines these questions.

4 Fascism, Nihilism and Egotism

Fascism has often been called an anti-ideology; and possibly its significance lies not in any positive achievements but in its negativity and destructiveness. Indeed it was bound to fail in the end. It depended too much on fallible - very fallible - human beings. Rudolf Hess (deputy Führer 1933-39) said of Hitler that he was 'pure reason in human form', and Robert Ley (the labour leader) called him 'the only man who never errs'.[8] But this was nonsense. Such hero-worship was even less realistic in the case of Mussolini. Once the Italian leader became a dictator, he lost all touch with real people: increasingly he was praised in ever more excessive terms and was told not the truth but what he wanted to hear. When an old colleague warned him of the dangers of ruling in isolation, Mussolini replied that he was immune from the vainglory and self-deceit which were the occupational hazards of dictators - and he then went on to compare himself to the heroic figures of the past and to call himself 'the invincible Duce'![9] He was being fooled by his own propaganda. Power, as Lord Acton said, tends to corrupt, and absolutely power corrupts absolutely - one of the few generalisations about human history which holds true.

Fascism may have begun as, in some respects, a real political ideology; but it became far less coherent once the dictators made it their own and subordinated it to their egotism. There is no doubt that Hitler and Mussolini were egotists: they cared only for themselves and felt contempt for other people. This was seen in its most extreme form in Hitler's hatred for the Jews, but in fact he despised all non-Germans. For instance, he said that those Poles who were not killed in the war should be mentally enfeebled: drink and pornographic literature were to be made available cheaply to them. Yet, despite his belief in the superiority of the Aryan master-race, he also had contempt for Germans. 'The mass of the working class,' he said, referring to his own people, 'want nothing but bread and games. They will never understand the meaning of an ideal'.[10] This lack of concern was even more apparent during the war. (Britain's wartime leader, Winston Churchill, was, perhaps, equally an egotist; but at least he was easily moved to tears by the suffering of others.) Hitler had no compunction in ordering that German soldiers who retreated should be shot. General Halder, who was chief of the army general staff from 1938 to 1942, judged that Germany did not really exist for Hitler: 'for him there was - at first subconsciously, but in his last years fully consciously - only one greatness, a greatness which dominated his life and to which his evil genius sacrificed everything - his own Ego.'[11] Some believe that the creation of a racially pure state was the driving force behind Hitler; but it is at least possible that his racial theories were in reality little more than a twisted rationalisation of his own sadistic impulses and embodiment of his own love of power. According to Bullock, the 'sole theme of the Nazi revolution was domination, dressed up as the doctrine of race'.[12] If this is so, then his fascism was essentially nihilistic (wantonly, mindlessly destructive).

Mussolini's attitude was similar. He said that he aimed to restore Italian greatness, but in reality he felt boundless contempt for all Italians except himself. The general public, he once insisted, 'are stupid, dirty, do not work hard enough and are content with their little cinema shows'.[13] Governing them, he judged, was not difficult but merely futile.

> When the masses are like wax in my hands, when I stir their faith, or when I mingle with them ... I feel myself to be a part of them. All the same there persists in me a certain feeling of aversion, like that which the modeller feels for the clay he is moulding. Does not the sculptor sometimes smash his block of marble into fragments?[14]

The fascist dictators had no more genuine regard for any human life, except of course their own, than had Stalin - or Atilla the Hun.

Fascism's doctrine of perpetual struggle left a legacy of Europe in ruins. Admittedly previous German and Italian governments had pursued adventures in foreign policy (after all, as A.J.P. Taylor once remarked, 'Power will be Powers', just as boys will be boys), but Hitler and Mussolini went much further than their predecessors. Hitler in fact had approved of the destruction in the First World War, though not of the German defeat, and he seems to have gloried in the mass destruction of the Second. Perhaps there was even some sort of death-wish at the heart of Nazism. Hitler mused in February 1942 that total defeat would be the best result, if Germany could not be victorious:

> All in all, it is surely best for someone who has no heir to whom to bequeath his house to be burned in it with all its contents - a magnificent funeral pyre![15]

His destructive legacy may be judged from two quotations from the diaries of Patrick Gordon Walker, a British observer of Germany at the end of the war. The first is a joke, an example of black humour, that was being told among the Britons in Germany:

> End of the war. Allied troops enter Berlin. Goering is seen trying to hide. Goebbels is trying to hobble off. Suddenly a man appears in a raincoat, tears off his little moustache and says: 'British secret agent no. 123 reporting. Mission completed. Germany destroyed.'[16]

The second, a description of Belsen prison camp, shows the full horrors of the Nazi regime:

> Got to Belsen. It is a vast area surrounded by barbed-wire. ... Next day some men of the Oxfordshire Yeomanry arrived. People crowded round them kissing their hands and feet and dying from weakness. Corpses in every stage of decay were lying around, piled up on top of each other in heaps. There were corpses in the compounds, in the blocks. People were falling dead all around, people who were walking skeletons. One woman came up to the soldier who was guarding the milk-store and doling out milk to children and begged for milk for her baby. The man took the baby and saw it had been dead for days - black in the face and shrivelled up. The mother went on begging for milk - so he poured some into its dead lips. The mother then gibbered and crooned with joy (the soldier's own words) - and carried the baby off in triumph. She stumbled and fell dead in a few yards. ... I walked all round the camp. Everywhere the smell and odour of death. After a few hours you get used to it and don't notice it any more. ...
>
> There are a very large number of girls in the compound, mostly Jewesses from Auschwitz. They have to be healthy to have survived. Over and over again I was told the same story - of the parades at which people stood naked for hours and were picked out arbitrarily (allegedly incapable of work) for the gas chambers and crematoriums, where many were burnt alive. ... At Auschwitz every woman had her hair shaved absolutely bald - many twice. I met pretty young girls whose hair was one inch long. They all had their numbers tattooed on their left arm. A mark of honour they will wear all their lives. ...
>
> I talked afterwards to a Dutch girl, Hetty Werkendamm, 15 years old, and her young brother. They had been 14 months in the

> camp. Their father and mother had worked in the workshop (where people were driven and beaten, and died in hordes). Their mother had to get up at 3 to try and get some food for the husband to eat whilst he was at work. Their father had gone to work one day with a scarf around his neck. The SS men in charge had, out of sheer fun, taken hold of the ends of the scarf and half strangled him. The little girl's stories went on endlessly: 'Once my father had to work,' she said, '- please excuse my language (she was a girl of 15) in the shit-pit. Right up to his arms, shovelling out the shit - I saw him when he came back from work.' Their mother and father had been taken away a month or so before. They were asking every officer they saw - 'How can we find out where our parents are?'[17]

The Nazis had insisted that they were creating a 'new man': instead, as Churchill said, they were threatening to unleash a new dark age. They showed how fragile is human civilisation.

5 Conclusion

Fascism cannot be assigned any simple significance. It was not the creation - or the tool - of wealthy capitalists or of any particular social class. Nor can we say that, in its effects, it was definitely modernising or reactionary: it was too complex a phenomenon to be assigned any such label. Many historians would agree that it was, up to a point, totalitarian. Insofar as this is true, fascism was unprincipled opportunism and power politics: it was a style of rule, devoid of genuine principles or ultimate aims. Its object was simply power for its own sake. Or was fascism purposeful? Many have argued that the fanatical quest for racial purity was the essential aim of Nazism. Yet if this is true, then Nazism stands in sharp contrast to Italian Fascism. After all, no one could realistically argue that Mussolini's *raison d'être* was the purification of Italian blood. A comic figure in many ways, Mussolini nevertheless retained far more sanity on this issue than Hitler. Perhaps therefore we should cease speaking of Nazism as fascist. Or, perhaps, as some have insisted, Hitler's was the archetypal fascist regime, so that the Fascists were not really, or not sufficiently, fascist. 'The Fascists were not fascist': this sounds like a contradiction in terms. Yet it is at least worth considering, especially since most fascist-like parties, especially in central and eastern Europe, were much more anti-Semitic than the Italians. Even so, many will be tempted to conclude that fascism is a conundrum.

So far we have focused on fascism as an 'epochal' (belonging to a particular epoch, that of the 1918-45 period) and a continental (European) movement. Yet perhaps the real significance of fascism is that it was - and still is - a much more wide-ranging, multi-faceted phenomenon. Some historians believe that interwar fascist groups were not confined to Europe, and moreover many insist that fascism survived the Axis defeat in 1945.

Many 'candidates' from outside 1918-45 Europe have been put forward for acceptance as fascist:

i) Perhaps Japan in the 1930s should be considered a fascist Power. After all, Japan - after the attack on the American fleet at Pearl Harbor in December 1941 - was the ally of Germany and Italy during the war. In addition, the regime was undemocratic and in many ways regimented its citizens. It was also highly nationalistic, militaristic, imperialist and racist. On the other hand, there was no fascist party, and Japanese authoritarianism - building on the legacy of the past - seemed so different from Europe's that some scholars have coined the term 'Japanism' to describe it.

ii) The wave of right-wing dictatorships in countries like Argentina (ruled by Juan Peron in 1946-55 and 1973-74), Chile (led by General Pinochet in 1973-89), Brazil and Bolivia have been called 'South American fascism'. Sometimes these military dictators are bracketed with the fascist-like rule of the 'Greek Colonels' (Papadopoulos and Pattakos, who ruled from 1967 to 1974).

iii) Many other dictatorships, for instance that of Nkrumah in Ghana (1957-66) and present-day regimes like that of Gadhafi in Libya and Saddam Hussein ('The Hitler of our time') in Iraq, have been called fascist, often because of their brutality and the 'cult of personality' built round the leader. Warring factions in the former Yugoslavia are also sometimes dubbed as fascist, especially for their racial antagonisms. The Serbian notion of 'ethnic cleansing' bears a chilling resemblance to the Nazis' 'final solution'.

iv) Despite the prosperity and materialism of Western Europe after the Second World War, neo-fascist groups have sprung up in this area. Examples include the National Front in Britain, the Front National led by Jean-Marie Le Pen in France, and the MSI (the Italian Socialist Movement - now part of the National Alliance). Most of these attempt to whip up popular opinion not against the Jews but against black immigrants. In 1989 a commission calculated that there were 69 extremist or neo-Nazi organisations in West Germany. So far these have been marginal groups, but there is no guarantee that they will remain so. Several commentators are profoundly worried that Russia, where economic problems are so profound, may eventually succumb to some modern variant of fascism now that the Soviet regime has collapsed.

This information prompts two comments. First, if so many diverse regimes are accepted as being fascist (and there is no agreement on this issue), the meaning of the term is stretched more and more widely and so becomes an even more formidable conundrum. Any study of 'fascism' must therefore begin and end with the problem of definition (to which we return in the final chapter). Second, no ultimate significance can be assigned to fascism: future developments may radically affect the judgements of historians. We are too close to fascism to see it whole and understand it fully.

References

1 Stanley G. Payne, *A History of Fascism 1914-45* (UCL Press, 1995), p. 127.
2 Niall Rothnie, *National Socialism in Germany* (Macmillan, 1987), p. 33.
3 Denis Mack Smith, *Mussolini* (Granada, 1981), p. 160.
4 Philip Morgan, *Italian Fascism* (Macmillan, 1995), p. 80.
5 Franz Neumann, *Behemoth* (Gollancz, 1942), p. 47.
6 Payne, *History of Fascism*, p. 123.
7 George Orwell, *Nineteen Eighty-Four* (Penguin, 1954), p. 212.
8 J.P. Stern, *Hitler: The Fuhrer and the People* (Flamingo, 1984), p. 111.
9 Mack Smith, *Mussolini*, p. 236
10 O. Strasser, *Hitler and I* (Cape, 1940), p. 117.
11 Alan Bullock, *Hitler: A Study in Tyranny* (Penguin, 1962), p. 775.
12 Ibid, p. 804.
13 Mark Robson, *Italy: Liberalism and Fascism 1870-1945* (Hodder and Stoughton, 1992), p. 76.
14 Stern, *Hitler*, p. 45
15 Hugh Trevor-Roper (ed), *Hitler's Table-Talk* (OUP, 1988), p. 316.
16 Robert Pearce (ed), *Patrick Gordon Walker: Political Diaries, 1932-1971* (The Historians' Press, 1991), p. 122.
17 Ibid., pp. 143-4, 146-9.

Answering essay questions on *'The Significance of Fascism'*

Consider the following questions:

1 To what extent should fascism be called a revolutionary force in Europe from 1918 to 1945?
2 Should both Fascist Italy and Nazi Germany be described as totalitarian states?
3 'The puppets of the capitalists.' Discuss this view of Hitler and Mussolini.

Think how you might write a final paragraph for each of these questions. Remember that in your conclusion you should be pulling together the strands of your argument and summing up your overall answer to the question set as directly, clearly and forcefully as you can. (It is as well to be aware of what you should not be doing: do not bring in new factual information at this stage or a new interpretation inconsistent with what you have already written; and do not address the 'next' topic, having already finished answering the question set.)

Try writing 6-8 sentences on the above titles. Such a limited number should force you to keep to the point. For the first question, you must decide the extent to which the fascist regimes were revolutionary, and you may wish to distinguish not just between different regimes but

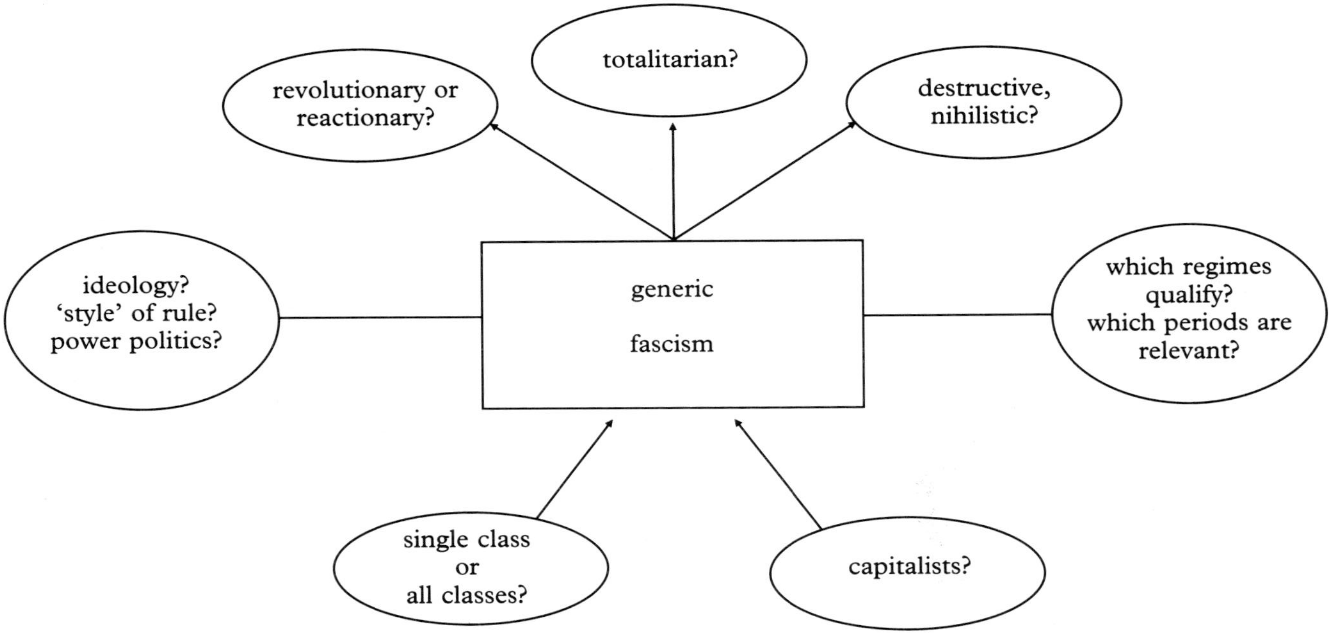

Summary - The Significance of Fascism

between their revolutionary nature at different times or in different areas of their impact. In short, the final paragraph should be your overall argument. Hence, in your essay-writing, you might well decide in future to write the last paragraph first. This is a technique that may work for you: at least it should ensure that your essays are internally consistent rather than self-contradictory.

For number 2, you should end by saying either 'Yes' or 'No', though this may well need to be qualified, for instance by 'in certain respects' or 'at particular times' in order to bring out the extent of their totalitarianism. Don't forget that you are asked about both regimes, and therefore if you think that only one of the regimes was totalitarian your answer should be 'No, but ...' Question 3 is an open-ended discussion: this gives you a great deal of scope, and so you can conclude with any form of words, providing that they add up to a relevant argument.

CHAPTER 6

Conclusion: The Meanings of Fascism

This book started with a series of questions about fascism (a-h on pages 4-6), culminating in the key issue of how the term is best defined. Now is the time to formulate at least tentative conclusions.

a) Why did so many fascist parties and regimes exist in the interwar period?

This question has been analysed in chapters 2 and 3. We have seen that proto-fascism grew up in Europe before 1914 and that the First World War provided ideal circumstances for it to flourish. In the postwar years there were important problems (including communist threats, nationalist grievances, economic dislocation and democratic weakness) which enabled fascists to attract support, and moreover there were groups of ex-servicemen who were ready recruits to their para-military groups. Yet fascism stemmed not only from common, European-wide factors but from historical traditions and contingent factors which, by their very nature, were unique to particular situations. Once Mussolini and Hitler came to power, they sponsored fascist parties elsewhere, but often their efforts were counter-productive, since it was essential that fascist groups appeared to be genuinely local responses to national grievances. Given that fascists were so nationalistic, 'international fascism' is, in many ways, a contradiction in terms. Certainly there were bound to be significant variations between different fascist groups: the key question is how much variation can there be before the label 'fascist', by obscuring local differences, hinders historical understanding.

Full understanding of the growth of fascism demands a consideration of the psychologies of those who supported it, a fascinating area but one which, so far, has not yielded generally acceptable explanations. Notions of a particular 'authoritarian personality' attracted to fascism have failed to convince. Nor do general psychological explanations help us understand the timing of the dictators' rise to power. Nevertheless, explaining the emergence of right-wing groups in particular countries is relatively straightforward. Much more complicated, however, is our second question.

b) Exactly which regimes should be called fascist?

A large number of regimes have been called fascist, but we saw in chapter 3 that many of the authoritarian right-wing regimes of the interwar period - especially in central, southern and eastern Europe - did not call themselves fascist and are generally considered to be military or monarchical dictatorships, often buttressed ideologically by Catholicism. Hence they were more conservative than fascist. Sometimes, in their quest for power, they used dissident fascist groups, as Franco took advantage of the Falange, but always they were distinct from them, as was Horthy from Szálasi's Arrow Cross Party in Hungary or Salazar from Preto's National Syndicalists in Portugal. In Italy and Germany, however, the opposite happened: the fascists successfully used the conservatives, as Mussolini took advantage of Giolitti and Hitler manipulated von Papen.

The concept of generic fascism therefore seems to stand or fall by the degree of similarity between only two regimes, Fascist Italy and Nazi Germany. Does it make sense to call them both 'fascist'? It is possible to interpret the differences between them as merely *quantitative* (differences of degree), with Nazi Germany as simply a more efficient - or Germanic - version of Fascist Italy. Perhaps the variations between the two regimes reflect the different resources and historical traditions of the two countries (in terms of political cultures, economic strength and social structures). The Nazi regime penetrated more deeply into people's lives, but then there were more traditions of state intervention here than in Italy. Germany was a more advanced industrial society, and therefore more efficient tools of social control were at hand. In Italy, in contrast, the central government had traditionally been viewed with suspicion, especially in the poorer but more independent south. The Church was also stronger in Italy. If the differences between the two regimes can be explained in this fashion, then the concept of generic fascism survives. Hitler and Mussolini were undoubtedly similar, especially to the extent that the Führer was, as some have insisted, a 'weak dictator'.

Yet there are degrees of weakness, and Hitler was not weak in all respects. In addition, there are significant differences between Fascism and Nazism. Compare, for instance, the OVRA and the SS. They seem similar in that both had the same function, that of terrorising enemies of the regimes, but their actions - and the terror they inspired - were very different. Similarly both Germany and Italy fought in the Second World War, but look at the enormous contrast between their performances. Most important of all is Hitler's anti-Semitism, which was so different from that pursued, without resolution, in Italy. Does the contrast here amount only to a difference in degree or to a stark difference in kind? If there was a *qualitative* difference, then generic fascism may be a misleading term.

Weighing up the similarities and differences between the two regimes depends very much on which ingredients we put into the scales and how much significance we assign to each. Hence no two judges are likely to reach exactly the same conclusion. Several contrasting verdicts are contained in the evidence below.

Consider this extract from a speech Mussolini made when in Berlin in

September 1937, in which he stressed the similarities between Nazism and Fascism:

> I have come among you in my capacity as head of a national revolution who has wanted to give proof of open and unequivocal solidarity with your revolution. And even if the course of the two revolutions has not been the same, the objective which both wanted to achieve, and have achieved, is the same: the unity and greatness of the people. ...
>
> Just as fifteen years of Fascism have given a new material and spiritual countenance to Italy, so your revolution has given a new face to Germany: new, even if, as in Italy, it is based on the most noble and eternal traditions which can be reconciled with the necessities of modern life ...
>
> We have many elements of *Weltanschauung* [philosophical outlook on the world] in common. Not only have Nazism and Fascism everywhere the same enemies who serve the same masters, the Third International [the Comintern], but they share many conceptions of life and history. Both believe in violence as a force determining the life of peoples, as the dynamo of their history, and hence reject the doctrines of so-called historical materialism and their political and philosophical by-products. Both of us exalt work in its countless manifestations as the sign of the nobility of man; both of us count on youth, from which we demand the virtues of discipline, courage, tenacity, patriotism, and scorn for the comfortable life. ...[1]

There is some obvious humbug here. Mussolini was impressed with German power and wanted to be on the winning side in any future war. But was it all humbug?

Consider also Hitler's words while at dinner on 23 April 1942:

> I hold the Duce in the highest esteem, because I regard him as an incomparable statesman. On the ruins of a ravished Italy he has succeeded in building a new State which is a rallying point for the whole of his people. The struggles of the Fascists bear a strong resemblance to our own struggles. ... The Duce is one of the few people who appreciated the full measure of the Bolshevik menace, and for this reason he has sent to our Eastern front divisions of real military merit. He told me himself that he had no illusions as to the fate of Europe if the motorised hordes of the Russian armies were allowed to sweep unchecked over the Continent, and he is quite convinced that, but for my intervention, the hour of decline was approaching for western Europe.[2]

Hitler, paying Mussolini the greatest compliment he ever paid anyone, once said that the Duce was 'almost equal to myself'.[3] Yet in 1943 Himmler insisted that 'Fascism and National Socialism are two fundamentally different things. ... There is absolutely no comparison between Fascism and National Socialism as spiritual, ideological movements.' Goebbels added that 'Mussolini is not a revolutionary like the Führer or Stalin'.[4]

The cartoonist David Low certainly saw important differences between Hitler and Mussolini. He satirised the latter consistently as 'Muzzler the Dictator', as in the drawings over the page; but whereas he at first saw Hitler as a similarly ridiculous figure, he soon changed his mind. The cartoons (on page 116), from June 1933 and July 1934, show his stark reinterpretation of the Nazi leader.

Clearly there was no identity between Fascism and Nazism. If therefore we use the common adjective 'fascist' to describe them, this term - while denoting significant similarities between the regimes - must also be allowed to imply significant differences as well. We all have to make up our own minds on the balance. Was there a 'family resemblance' between them?

c) Was fascism a political ideology?

This question was considered in chapter 2. There are indeed common ideas associated with the leading fascist movements, including struggle, anti-democracy and anti-communism. Biological racism was also a component of the thinking of many of those who called themselves, or have been called, fascists. The leadership principle also came to be commonly associated with fascism in the interwar years, though it was not always present before this time. Yet this *Führerprinzip* may seem to make nonsense of the coherence of fascism as an ideology. How can one take fascist philosophy seriously when the great leader can reverse policy whenever he chooses?

Some hotly deny that fascism is an ideology. Yet, of course, it all depends how 'ideology' is defined. What degree of coherence must ideas have before the word is justified? This is a good question - but an unanswerable one. All we can say is that if fascism is an ideology, it must be considered one of the loosest, vaguest and least coherent. It does not qualify in any but a weak sense because its ideas were not logical or consistent enough. At its centre was not reason but (Sorelian) myth, especially the myth of national greatness and the myth of the infallible leader.

Yet perhaps the ideological issue is a red herring and we should concentrate instead on the more neutral 'concept' or 'doctrines' of fascism. We can be certain that there were characteristic fascist ideas, and perhaps these constitute a 'lowest common denominator' or fascist 'minimum': for instance, fascists must always be authoritarian and nationalistic (and perhaps other features should be added to the list).

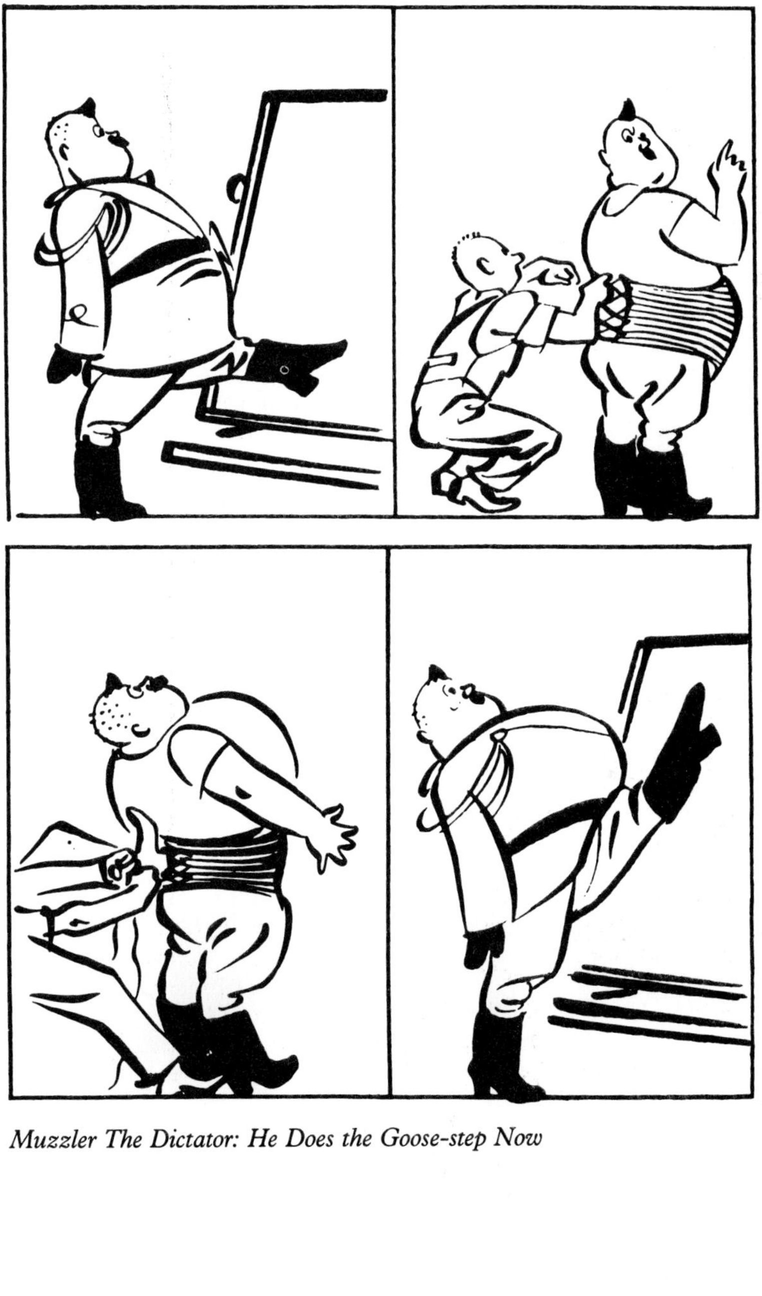

Muzzler The Dictator: He Does the Goose-step Now

All Blown Up And Nowhere To Go

They Salute With Both Hands Now

Some argue that this commonality of ideas justifies the concept of generic fascism. But we must be certain what they mean by this argument. They do not mean that all fascist movements were the same or even that, in their basic policies, they were similar. All they mean is that the fascists shared certain common ideas - ideas which may or may not have significantly influenced their actions and achievements. Hence the fascist 'minimum' is very low indeed. In short, generic fascism is a 'taxonomic device' (a means of classification). It groups certain parties and regimes together on the basis of the ideas they had in common. Yet since these movements had differences as well as similarities, this cannot be the only means of classifying them, and nor is it necessarily the best.

Many of us would accept that, on this definition, there was such a thing as generic fascism. But some believe that if the differences between the fascists outweighed their similarities, then the concept is not particularly useful. In particular political historians tend to insist that we should not look merely at ideas but also at actions.

d) Was fascism a 'style' of rule?

Perhaps what distinguishes fascism is the political theatre associated with it. There is something to be said for this idea. Certainly there was a characteristic style of fascist rule, often resulting from the ways in which the fascists attempted to impress and indoctrinate the masses. Mass rallies, militaristic parades, political symbols, the cult of the leader, 'fancy dress', extensive control of the mass media - all these were aspects of fascism. Yet if the essence of fascism was merely a style of rule, as was perhaps the case in Italy, then this shows its basic emptiness of achievement. It should also be noted that if this was its essence, then perhaps many monarchical and military dictatorships qualify as being fascist. On the other hand, it must be asked whether non-fascist states, including the USSR, also employed similar techniques of control. Insofar as they did, fascism cannot be defined as a specific style of rule.

e) Was fascism the tool of the capitalists?

Generic fascism is such a complex subject that we all have moments in which we long for a simple explanation of it - as, for instance, that the fascist dictators were the agents of wealthy capitalists. Yet this theory will not do. (At its most bizarre, it has taken the form of a Jewish conspiracy: wealthy Jews, who dominated finance, are said to have created fascism.) Certainly it cannot be objectively proven that capitalism spawned fascism, although individual capitalists were instrumental in the rise of both Hitler and Mussolini. Nor can it be shown that only a single class supported the fascists. For a time the petty bourgeoisie may have been their most characteristic supporters and voters, but this simply showed that they were susceptible to fascist propaganda: it does not necessarily tell us much about the essential nature of fascism. Certainly the dictators subsequently let down their lower middle class supporters: their regimes benefited not the small independent trader but large-scale capitalism - at least before the mass destruction of the Second World War.

f) Was fascism similar to totalitarianism?

The answer, as so often with historical questions, is yes and no. It depends of course on what we mean by 'similar' - as well as 'totalitarianism' and 'fascism'! As early as 1926 Luigi Sturzo defined Bolshevism as 'left Fascism' and Fascism as 'right Bolshevism'.[5] This was going too far, since it takes no account whatsoever of the different ideas and goals associated with communism. Yet there were definite parallels between fascism and Stalin's communism, and insofar as fascism was merely a style of rule or a system of power politics - devoid of real ideological principles - then these similarities seem particularly significant. No doubt Fernández-Armesto is correct to judge that the politics of twentieth-century Europe are horseshoe-shaped, so that 'the extremists at both ends seemed close enough to touch'. Certainly from the perspective of the future, 'the differences between all forms of violent political extremism will blur'.[6] Fascism and communism were not identical, but they can - for purposes of classification (taxonomy) - be represented as sub-divisions of totalitarianism.

g) What was the nature of fascist regimes?

Any simple answer to this question is bound to seem simplistic. An evaluation of fascist regimes hinges on which aspects of their rule we focus on, and at which particular times. In addition, there is the added difficulty of deciding which particular activities were specifically fascist. For instance, the holocaust was a vitally important part of Nazism, but anti-Semitism was not part of Fascist philosophy and, some would argue, does not form part of the fascist 'minimum'. Equally significantly, the only two states which are generally called fascist - Italy and Germany - performed startlingly differently, especially during the Second World War. Hence the 'nature' - i.e. the essential characteristics - of fascist regimes are seemingly impossible to define. Some have seen them as developmental dictatorships, modernising their states, but there is no general consensus on this issue. So much depends, for instance, on our definition of 'modernism'. (Is mass regimentation specifically modern?)

Nevertheless it is at least worth considering the view that the fascist regimes were inherently unstable because, on several levels, they were contradictory. For instance, they aimed to utilise science and technology to promote development and efficiency, and yet science ('think logically and creatively') and the leadership principle ('follow the leader') were incompatible. Even the elite schools in Germany did not have particularly high standards - physical excellence, yes, but not intellectual excellence. In addition, many fascist-like dogmas (for instance about race) were simply untrue. Similarly the fascist leaders were incapable of living up to the superhuman images of themselves that they helped to create. From the perspective of 1945, it seemed that the nature of fascism had been first destructive and then self-destructive.

1 Conclusion

h) How is fascism best defined?

This is the final question and easily the most important. It is also the most difficult. There are two basic ways of approaching it. The first is that of people who like to lay down the law. They perceive some sort of 'essence' (or at least lowest common denominator) in fascism and insist that this is the correct way of defining it: all other ways are simply wrong. The second seeks to avoid such prescriptive judgements and insists that there is no objectively correct definition of fascism: words are defined by their usages - by the meanings which we give them.

If we adopt the first method, and define fascism in our own particular way (for instance as totalitarianism or as a combination of precise characteristics), we are ignoring the fact that words are used in different ways and we run the risk of selecting from the huge variety of the past only those aspects which fit in with our view. (We are also likely to be branded as fascist for trying to foist our view on other people!) If we adopt the second, however, we are faced with the dilemma that the word fascism has been used so diversely that we will end up accepting mutually incompatible definitions. Hence we must steer a course between the two - somehow.

First, we should reject those interpretations which clearly do not fit the facts. For instance, there was no paradigm (essential, perfect version) of fascism. Neither Fascist Italy nor Nazi Germany qualifies as this sort of model. Nor was fascism a monolithic - or fully unified - movement which stalked Europe in the interwar period and which was 'at home everywhere', as Thomas Mann feared (see page 1). Certainly the similarities between Fascist Italy and Nazi Germany are not so exact that the two regimes can be seen as two sides of the same fascist coin. Indeed no two fascist parties, let alone regimes, were the same. Generic fascism was in fact heterogeneous (diverse) rather than homogeneous (of a single kind). Its essential nature was that it had no absolutely essential nature: it was simply the sum of its parts, and these parts were varied, so that we might even distinguishing between different types of fascism. Therefore we must try to work out not the meaning but the *meanings* of fascism (hence the title of this chapter).

The four following views of fascism are worth considering:

i) Generic fascism did not exist. Instead, there was in Europe a series of separate movements with little in common between them. Admittedly, some regimes used similar and undemocratic techniques to rule their people: but then throughout history regimes have used the most up-to-date means available. (Why would they do anything else?) As for the political ideas associated with 'fascism', such a rag-bag of half-baked clichés could not possibly form the basis of a Europe-wide movement. The most consistent doctrine associated with fascism is that of Nazi racism, but in fact this had nothing to do with generic fascism. Nazism was unique. Italian Fascism was also unique.

ii) Fascism was really just a twentieth-century version of power politics. As Oswald Mosley wrote, it was 'Science and Caesarism',[7] the rule of one man using the most up-to-date methods of controlling his country and determining its policies. Or, in the words of Felipe Fernández-Armesto, it was 'just a slick name for unprincipled opportunism'.[8] Hence it was a style of rule plus totalitarian methods. According to this view, all the noble fascist rhetoric about self-sacrifice and rebirth gave way before the egotism of the dictators. Hitler talked about will-power, and some have mistakenly seen will as part of fascist philosophy, but in reality it was nothing but egotism (the modern equivalent of Julius Caesar's 'I came, I saw, I conquered'). There can be little doubt that dictators like Mussolini and Hitler were power-hungry tyrants, and as such were no new phenomenon. ('Power!' Hitler screamed in one of his first meetings with Otto Strasser, in the 1920s; 'Power first! Afterwards we can act as circumstances dictate!'[9])

iii) Generic fascism has meaning because of the hard core of common ideas (vitalist, nationalistic, anti-positivist and social Darwinist) which the fascists had in common. Admittedly the dictators were not always serious about some of the ideas they propounded, but then they were not political philosophers. The important thing is that the doctrines preceded the dictators. It is this common link which gives meaning to generic fascism. Fascism is thus a matter essentially of ideas.

iv) Fascism is not just a matter of ideology or doctrine. The fascists were not chair-bound theorists; they believed in action. They actually attempted to put into practice their anti-communism, their hatred of democracy and their commitment to violence. Indeed the extent to which these ideas were acted upon determined the degree to which parties or regimes were fascist. Hence some regimes were fascist in a relatively strong sense, while others qualify only in the weakest of senses - and, with the latter, the deployment of the term will be a matter of judgement, and often of very fine judgement. But in no case will the label 'fascist' be an exclusive judgement, since other adjectives will also be applicable. For instance, Hitler's regime can be described as Nazi, totalitarian or racist as well as fascist.

As students of fascism, we can agree with any of these four broad options - providing we have good reasons. But it is also worth considering whether it is possible to agree with them all, at least to some degree. Can they be combined?

The first view insists that Nazism and Fascism were unique (or *sui generis*). Everyone will surely accept this. But this does not mean that they were different in every single respect. Clearly they did have things in common; and even if we judge that their differences outweighed their similarities, these points of contact may provide the building blocks of generic fascism. The second view points to one such similarity, their emphasis on power and on the means of retaining that power, so that fascism can be seen either as a form of totalitarianism or as something very closely allied to it. Thirdly, there were common doctrines between the different fascist groups, so that generic fascism may refer to the ideas they had in common. Indeed many philosophers and historians of ideas endorse the notion that such links provide a perfectly satisfactory explanation of generic fascism. Political historians, however, tend to judge that fascism was bogus unless it affected the real world of actions and achievement. Hence they tend to adopt a 'check list' approach (see page 10) to match the multi-faceted character of fascism. The fourth option insists that, to some extent, ideas did influence action and therefore fascism was a reality.

Various historians have had the courage to provide their own definitions of this enigmatic term. Consider that of the doyen of the historians of fascism, Stanley Payne. In his view fascism can be defined as

> a form of revolutionary ultra-nationalism for national rebirth that is based on a primarily vitalist philosophy, is structured on extreme elitism, mass mobilization, and the *Führerprinzip*, positively values violence as end as well as means and tends to normalize war and/or the military virtues.[10]

Payne here gives no indication of the enormous variety exhibited by different fascist groups, while some of his terms - like 'extreme elitism' - themselves need defining. But of course no single sentence can possibly be adequate. (Sometimes two sentences, like two heads, are better than one.) But this definition does bring together the characteristic ideas of fascism, its forms of organisation, the important element of power politics (via the *Führerprinzip*) and fascist policies (like war). It may therefore be a better, more historically coherent, definition than those which stress some single feature.

Nevertheless the only way to define fascism fully is, as the Italian historian Tasca once said, 'to write its history'.[11] In short, we must focus not on the word but on the histories of the states which may be called fascist. There is no other way of solving the conundrum of fascism. After all, there can be no short-cut to understanding. No 'theory' or 'model', which are only simplifications of reality, will show us the truth. History is bigger, less predictable, more variable, and much more unfathomable - and therefore far more interesting - than any theory. Let the philosophers and theorists argue endlessly about the meaning of words; historians will not waste their time searching for terminological exactitude, especially when the term fascism is so ambiguous. Instead, we learn endlessly about the past until we begin to understand; and, once we do, the precise terms we use - and whether we deny or affirm the existence of 'generic fascism' - ceases to be such a difficult, or profoundly important, issue.

References

1 Roger Griffin (ed), *Fascism* (OUP, 1995), p. 79.
2 Hugh Trevor-Roper (ed), *Hitler's Table-Talk* (OUP, 1988), p. 437.
3 S.J. Woolf (ed), *European Fascism* (Weidenfeld and Nicolson, 1968), p. 29.
4 Stanley G. Payne, *A History of Fascism 1914-45* (UCL Press, 1995), p. 210.
5 Ibid, p. 447.
6 Felipe Fernández-Armesto, *Millennium* (Bantam Press, 1995), p. 482.
7 Oswald Mosley, *My Life* (Nelson, 1968), p. 316.
8 Fernández-Armesto, *Millennium,* p. 482.
9 O. Strasser, *Hitler and I* (Cape, 1940), p. 74.
10 Payne, *A History of Fascism,* p. 14.
11 Roger Griffin, *The Nature of Fascism* (Routledge, 1991), p. 21.

Source-based questions on *'Conclusion: The Meanings of Fascism'*

1 Mussolini and Hitler on fascism.

Read the extracts from Mussolini and Hitler on page 113. Answer the following questions:

a) What do you think Mussolini meant when he implied (lines 3-4) that 'the course of the two revolutions has not been the same'? (3 marks)
b) Mussolini insisted that the objective of the Fascist and Nazi revolutions was 'the unity and greatness of the people' (lines 5-6). Explain whether the Nazis would necessarily have agreed. (3 marks)
c) How many common ideas were shared by the two statements? (5 marks)
d) In what ways do Hitler's words show a misunderstanding of Mussolini and Italian Fascism? (5 marks)
e) Mussolini's words were delivered to a public audience, Hitler's were spoken at dinner. How may these different contexts affect our assessment of their reliability? (4 marks)

2 Low on the Dictators.

Study the cartoons on pages 115 and 116. Answer the following questions:

a) Sum up the essential message which Low is trying to put across in each of the cartoons. (5 marks)

b) Explain how the drawing of the dictator in each cartoon reinforces the message. (5 marks)

c) To what extent were Low's interpretation of Hitler and Mussolini justified by historical events and circumstances? (5 marks)

Chronological Table

1895		Karl Lueger's Christian Social Party gained control of Vienna
1899		Action Française founded by Maurras
1904		German Workers' Party founded in Bohemia
1905		Union of the Russian People founded
1909		the Futurists founded by Marinetti
1910		the ANI (Italian Nationalist Association) founded by Corradini
1915		Italy joined the First World War
1917	November	Bolshevik Revolution in Russia; battle of Caporetto
1918	9 November	abdication of Kaiser Wilhelm II
	11 November	end of the First World War
1919		Béla Kun's communist regime in Budapest
	January	Spartakist rising in Berlin
	March	Mussolini founded the Fascist movement (*Fasci di combattimento*)
	June	the Treaty of Versailles
	September	D'Annunzio seized Fiume
	November	Fascists did poorly in Italian elections: socialists became largest single party
1920		Horthy became regent in Hungary
	March	Kapp putsch in Berlin
1921	May	Fascists won 35 seats in Italy
	October	Mussolini founded the Fascist party (PNF - *Partito Nazionale Fascista*)
1922	July	left-wing general strike in Italy
	27-31 October	the March on Rome: Mussolini appointed prime minister
1923		military dictatorship of Primo de Rivera in Spain
	January	French occupation of the Ruhr began
	November	Nazi beer hall putsch in Munich; the Acerbo law in Italy
1924		Dawes plan re-scheduled reparations
	April	Fascists achieved majority in parliament; Fiume was ceded to Italy
	June	murder of Matteotti
1925	May	*Dopolavoro* created in Italy

1926		ONB created in Italy; Ministry of Corporations founded in Italy; Pilsudski came to power in Poland
1927		Battle for births launched in Italy; Iron Guard was founded in Romania
	July	rioting in Vienna, 88 killed
1928		Salazar became minister of finance, and later dictator, in Portugal
	May	Nazis won 2.5 per cent of votes in elections
1929		King Alexander set up dictatorship in Yugoslavia; Young plan scaled down reparations
	February	Lateran Treaty with the Papacy
1930	March	Müller's coalition collapsed in Germany
	September	Nazis won 107 seats in Reichstag
1931		Left-wing republican government in Spain
1932		creation of the British Union of Fascists; National Syndicalists set up in Portugal
	July	Nazis won 230 seats in the Reichstag
	November	Nazis won 196 seats in the Reichstag
1933		electoral victory for the right in Spain; Institute for Industrial Reconstruction set up in Italy
	30 January	Hitler became German Chancellor
	27 February	the Reichstag fire
	23 March	the Enabling Act was passed
	March	coup in Austria by Chancellor Dollfuss
1934		founding of Spanish Falange
	February	fighting in Vienna: at least 1,000 killed
	30 June	the Night of the Long Knives
	25 July	Nazi coup crushed in Austria: Dollfuss killed
	August	Hindenburg died: Hitler became Führer
	October	attempted left-wing revolution in Spain
1935	April	the Stresa front (Italy, Britain, France)
	October	Mussolini launched attack on Abyssinia
1936		formation of the French Popular Party; Popular Front won general election: beginning of civil war in Spain; Metaxas came to power in Greece
	September	start of Four Year Plan in Germany
1937		Franco merged Falange with the Carlists
1938		coup by King Carol II in Romania
	March	Hitler's forces invaded Austria: the *Anschluss*

1939	April	Mussolini invaded Albania; end of civil war in Spain
	May	the Pact of Steel (Germany and Italy)
	August	the Nazi-Soviet Pact
	September	start of Second World War
1940	10 June	Mussolini entered Second World War
1941	June	Hitler's invasion of the Soviet Union
	December	Japan bombed Pearl Harbor; Hitler declared war against the United States
1943	26 June	Mussolini was dismissed by the king
1945	28 April	Mussolini killed by Italian partisans
	30 April	suicide of Hitler in Berlin
	7 May	unconditional surrender of Germany
	15 August	unconditional surrender of Japan

Further Reading

A bewilderingly large number of books has been written on fascism, in its various guises. This short guide can therefore include no more than a brief selection of material. Those wishing to pursue more intensive research are advised to consult **Philip Rees**, *Fascism and Pre-Fascism in Europe, 1890-1945: A Bibliography of the Extreme Right* (Harvester Press, 1984) or the bibliography in **Stanley G. Payne's** *A History of Fascism* (see below), which runs to almost 2,000 items.

1 Europe in General

For an excellent brief study of aspects of interwar Europe, which puts fascism into a wide context, see **R.J. Overy**, *The Inter-War Crisis 1919-1939* (Longman, 1994). Also very valuable is **Stephen J. Lee**, *The European Dictatorships 1918-1945* (Routledge, 1987).

2 Generic fascism

The best single book is **Stanley G. Payne**, *A History of Fascism 1914-45* (UCL Press, 1995): a scholarly study of 600 pages, it is also very well written and surprisingly accessible. Much shorter, but in fact less readable, is **Alexander J. De Grand**, *Fascist Italy and Nazi Germany: The 'Fascist' Style of Rule* (Routledge, 1995). Also very valuable is **Roger Griffin**, *The Nature of Fascism* (Routledge, 1993 edition): written by a specialist in the history of ideas, it is complex but does repay detailed study; it also includes a very valuable glossary. A more straightforward account is provided by **Roger Eatwell**, *Fascism: A History* (Chatto & Windus, 1995). Eatwell's ideas have been summarised in 'What is Fascism?', two articles in the *History Review*, September and December 1996. A straightforward account of the origins of fascism has been provided by **F.L. Carsten**, *The Rise of Fascism* (Batsford, 1967). **Zeev Sternhell**, *The Birth of Fascist Ideology* (Princeton University Press, 1994), focuses on Italy and France.

Other important studies include **Renzo De Felice**, *Interpretations of Fascism* (Harvard University Press, 1977), which argues that fascism was essentially a movement of the ascendant petty bourgeoisie. He, like many other scholars, adopts a 'check-list' approach to fascism. This is much easier and more straightforward than **Ernst Nolte**, *Three Faces of Fascism* (Weidenfeld and Nicolson, 1965). **Alastair Hamilton**, *The Appeal of Fascism* (Anthony Blond, 1971) goes a long way towards explaining why so many intellectuals were attracted to fascism. For an analysis of Marxist ideas on fascism, see **David Beetham**, *Marxists in Face of Fascism* (Manchester University Press, 1983) and also **Martin Kitchen,** *Fascism* (Macmillan, 1976), whose author sees fascism as essentially 'an offensive against the working class'. A very useful book for its mass of information is **S. Larsen, B. Hagtvet and J. Myklebust (eds)**, *Who were the Fascists: Social Roots of European Fascism* (Universitets Forlaaget, Bergen, 1980).

On the complex and subtle relationship between fascists and conservatives, in a dozen countries, see **Martin Blinkhorn (ed)**, *Fascists and Conservatives* (Unwin Hyman, 1990). Blinkhorn's introduction provides an admirable survey: one of his conclusions is that the closeness of the two groups shows that fascism must be located on the right of the political spectrum. The essays themselves are of varying degrees of accessibility. So are those contained in **Richard Bessel (ed)**, *Fascist Italy and Nazi Germany* (CUP, 1996). An older collection provides a more uniformly valuable introduction: **S.J. Woolf (ed)**, *European Fascism* (Weidenfeld and Nicolson, 1968).

3 Italy

A very valuable introduction is provided by **Mark Robson**, *Italy: Liberalism and Fascism 1870-1945* (Hodder and Stoughton, 1992). Another fine introduction is provided by **Martin Blinkhorn**, *Mussolini and Fascist Italy* (Routledge, 2nd edition, 1994). For a fascinating overview of Mussolini's career, which is almost guaranteed to make students want to read more, see **Denis Mack Smith**, '"Sleeping-Car to Power": Mussolini's Italy 1922-1943', *Modern History Review*, November 1990. **Mack Smith's** biography *Mussolini* (Granada, 1983) is splendidly readable. More up-to-date, but far less entertaining, is **Philip Morgan**, *Italian Fascism* (Macmillan, 1995).

4 Germany

Books on Nazi Germany are legion. Two of the best introductions are provided by **Geoff Layton**, *Germany: The Third Reich* (Hodder and Stoughton, 1992) and **Dick Geary**, *Hitler and Nazism* (Routledge, 1993). An up-to-date account is given by **Ian Kershaw**, *The Nazi Dictatorship* (Edward Arnold, 3rd edition, 1993): this is not the easiest of books, but it repays detailed study and contains a very useful bibliography. Far more readable is **Alan Bullock**, *Hitler and Stalin: Parallel Lives* (HarperCollins, 1991), which also has a good bibliography.

5 Spain

Martin Blinkhorn, *Democracy and Civil War in Spain, 1931-1939* (Routledge, 1988) is a short but excellent introduction. Also valuable are **Harry Browne**, *Spain's Civil War* (Longman, 2nd edition, 1996),

Sheelagh Ellwood, *Franco* (Longman, 1993) and **Paul Preston**, *The Coming of the Spanish Civil War* (Routledge, 2nd edition, 1994).

6 Elsewhere

Books on particular countries include **Richard Thurlow**, *Fascism in Britain* (Blackwell, 1987), **Radu Iondid**, *The Sword of the Archangel: Fascist Ideology in Romania* (Boulder Colo., 1990), **F.L. Cartsen**, *Fascist Movements in Austria* (Sage, 1977), and **Robert Soucy**, *French Fascism* (New Haven, 1986). See also the articles in several of the collections above, especially **Woolf (ed)**, *European Fascism.*

7 Documents and Sources

The best collection is **Roger Griffin (ed)**, *Fascism* (OUP, 1995). Also valuable for material on Italy, Spain and Portugal is **Charles F. Delzell (ed)**, *Mediterranean Fascism, 1919-1945* (Harper & Row, 1970). **David Welch (ed)**, *Modern European History, 1871-1975* (Heinemann, 1994), has brief sections on Fascism and Nazism. Indispensable for Nazism are the 3 volumes edited by **J. Noakes and G. Pridham**, *Nazism 1919-1945* (University of Exeter Press, 1983-88).

Index

Major themes can be located from the Contents page